The Attitude Guy®

Peanut Butter

makes life better!

What My Fears, Flops And Failures Taught Me
About Finding Hope, Humor And Happiness

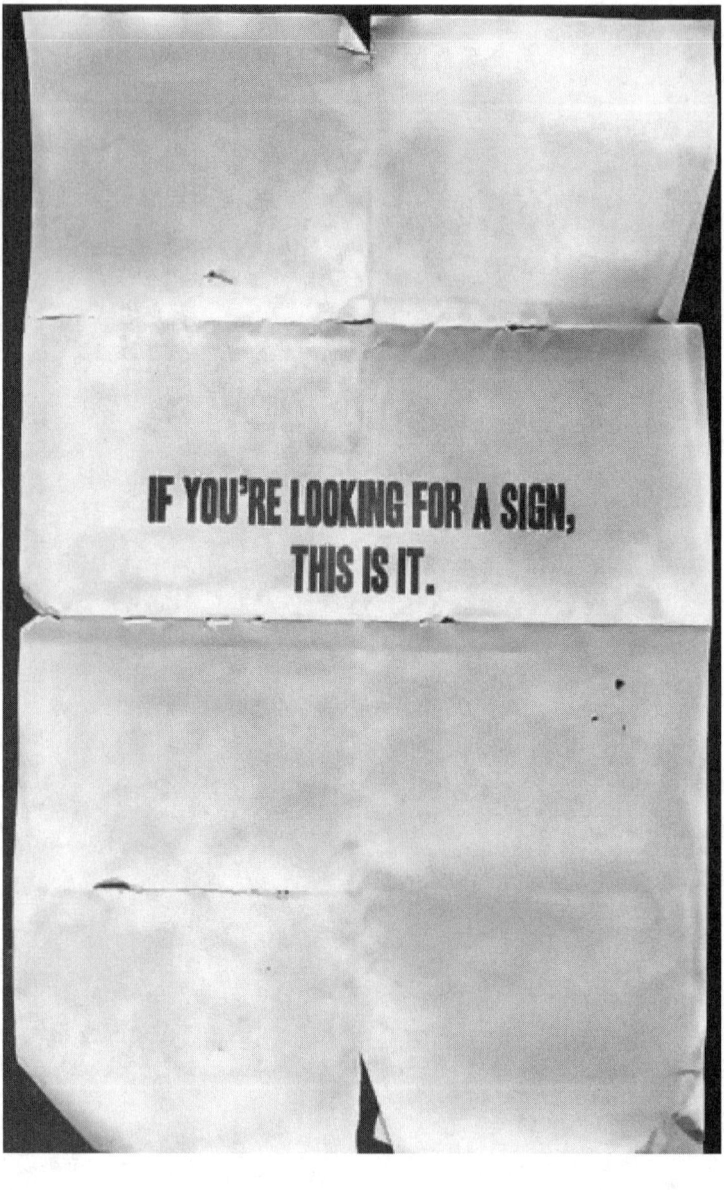
IF YOU'RE LOOKING FOR A SIGN,
THIS IS IT.

Peanut Butter Makes Life Better

What My Fears, Flops and Failures Taught Me about
Finding Hope, Humor and Happiness

Sam Glenn

The Attitude Guy ©

Published by Sam Glenn, Inc. 2014

ISBN 978-1-63452-010-2

Table of Contents

Praise for Peanut Butter
Makes Life Better

"This simple story of Sam Glenn's life experience is captivating, relatable, and very touching. I only put it down once to go get a spoon of peanut butter. Really! If you have struggled in your life with setbacks, lack of confidence, betrayals, or bad breaks, PB...MLB will encourage you!"

- *George Peintner*

"It always seems impossible until it's done."

Nelson Mandela

What to Expect In a Peanut Butter Nutshell...

I love stories that teach me humor that makes me laugh and good old fashioned positive encouragement that helps me grow. The following pages are filled with exactly that. This book is about strengthening your resilience, so that when life knocks you down and around, you can bounce back stronger than before and keep moving forward. The major portion of this book reveals some very personal stories regarding my own setbacks and battles with fear, failures, flops, guilt, shame, loss, negativity and some rash comments that I shouldn't be talking about in this sentence. I know…it's a lot, but some very encouraging and valuable lessons were learned from each encounter.

Speaking from personal experience, achieving

success is not as easy as it sometimes looks: anyone who thinks otherwise is delusional! Any worthy cause or ambition in life is going to require dedicated effort partnered with a positive attitude...that and lots of coffee. Please do not view this as a discouragement. It is just a fact. But, the other side of the coin is that when we find something worthy of our ambition, we become filled with enthusiasm, hope, meaning and purpose. Those are the things that fuel us to keep going. My study of history and pursuit of personal and professional success has convinced me that the road that leads us to achieving our desires is not easily navigable or smooth. Rather, it is a process of maneuvering through peaks and valleys. This is what makes the pursuit of what we want in life such an awesome adventure.

Throughout my own personal journey, I found hidden gifts and life lessons in what, at the time, seemed like adversities but later proved to be invaluable life lessons. Many times the gifts we receive are not readily apparent, but they eventually turn out for the best. It is said that life is meant to live going forward, but it makes more sense looking back. Gifts and life lessons hold special meanings that are unique to each of us depending on the season of "Life" we are experiencing at the time. Ideally, we can recognize these gifts and apply those lessons, so we are not distracted while we are trying our best to move forward. From the wounds and hurt feelings of our battles, we can uncover a new purpose and a renewed sense of ambition for life. This book deals with the unexpected happenings of life that can trip us up and what you can do to become more resilient, successful and happy. **To be happy and successful, we absolutely must learn and become resilient. That sentence alone may be worth underlining or writing out on a note card and posting it where you can see it every day.**

As you read through the following pages, my hope is that you feel an unexplainable surge of renewed strength. Perhaps, you will find that second wind you have been looking for that propels you to get up and try again.

Let me close this introduction by saying, despite the setbacks and crazy stories you are about to read, this book has a great ending: I can't wait to share it with you. But, don't skip to the end. If you read through my stories and get to know me, you will appreciate the final story. So, to get things rolling, let me kick things off with my favorite quote by the late Sir Edmond Hillary, who was the first explorer to reach the peak of Mt. Everest:

"It is not the mountain that we conquer, but ourselves."

Keep Moving Forward!

Sam Glenn, The Attitude Guy ©

www.SamGlenn.com

I Flunked Kindergarten, But Peanut Butter Saved the Day

Don't be too disappointed if you are a fan of peanut butter, because this book is actually not about peanut butter – well not that much. So, if you have a food allergy or think I might be pushing or promoting peanut butter as a source of betterment; I am not. I will say, in all honesty, that I absolutely love peanut butter. It's not just that it tastes good between two slices of bread or off the end of a spoon, but it also has some monumental meaning to me. Do I have praise for peanut butter? Could life go on without peanut butter? Yes, but not as pleasurably.

When I was in kindergarten (the first time), I guess I didn't do so well. I happen to believe that some kids learn differently. I was one of them.

My mom delayed the inevitable for as long as she could. She had to break the news to her six-year-old little boy. I was getting ready for a new school year and totally unaware what was about to hit me. Mom sat me down to have a talk. I got the vibe that it wasn't a "we are going to Disney World talk". Mom took a deep breath and began to explain that I would have to repeat kindergarten. At first, I didn't quite process the information as to exactly why I had to redo kindergarten. It took a few minutes for the message to sink in and then it hit me – I flunked kindergarten. My lower lip began to quiver and bubble out past the upper lip as you might see a little kid do when they are visibly upset and on the verge of crying. I asked what was wrong with me: why did I have to start kindergarten all over again? Mom explained as best as a young mother could, but even with her comforting words, it still hurt. I paused to think for a few minutes and then asked my mom if I was stupid. She paused for several hours to think about that question – just kidding! She didn't pause at all, and she did her best to reassure me that I was smart, talented and just needed a little extra time to learn and develop.

I am now in my 40's as I write this, and I can genuinely still recall the pain of that moment when I was just six years old. It was definitely a learning moment. I was so bummed out by this unexpected news that looking for the silver lining wasn't an immediate option for me, nor is it ever truly in life. We stew in the news and our mind gravitates to everything we think is wrong – about ourselves, life, work, people, the world, the situation and the list goes on. This is why teaching young people how to think in a more positive, healthy and constructive way in the face of unexpected adversities is so important. Today, organizations hire me to help create a better perspective as they face rapid changes and competition. So, that when the pressure of change is upon them, people will be more creative, innovative and make healthy and constructive choices.

After mom delivered the sad news that I was to repeat kindergarten, I wasn't in the mood to smile, play or be cheered up. I wanted to crawl under my bed and not come out. Mom tried her best to cheer me up by making some toast with peanut butter and a glass of cold milk. As I sat there eating the peanut butter toast, I actually started to feel a little better. I didn't feel great, but I felt better. I then broke my silence, *"Mom, I love peanut butter…. only the smooth kind though. It makes me feel better."* Mom just smiled.

Growing up, whenever I visit my parents' house (even to this day), I always make up some peanut butter toast. I sit at the kitchen table and reflect on things and every time I do, it gives me a sense of comfort and happiness. I don't indulge… *that much*, but it's that little thing in my life that brings me to a place of reflection, peace and calm. Life has a way of surprising us with "stuff" that can test our resolve, sink our happiness and deplete our hope. Let me ask you: what is your peanut butter – the one thing that brings you a little comfort and happiness? Everyone has something different. Now, I am not insinuating that at the end of a long and stressful week that you reach for unhealthy food or engage in unhealthy choices. Bad habits just make things worse. I am talking about that one thing, when life has bummed you out, that helps you find some clarity, focus, peace, serenity and happiness? I asked this question of a few people and they responded by saying their peanut butter was faith, art, tea or a good friend who listens and encourages. Others said reading a Sam Glenn book *(one of my favorites)*, going for a walk, watching an old funny movie, shopping (without credit cards), looking at family photos, snuggling with a favorite blanket, taking a hot shower, working out, golfing, fishing, painting and the list goes on and on. We all have our own peanut butter in life.

In this book, you will see peanut butter moments scattered throughout as I share my somewhat comical journey of flops, failures and fears and what they taught me about finding hope, humor and happiness.

So, why read or listen to someone who has failed, flopped and been afraid? I believe we can find an incredible amount of encouragement for our own situations in life by learning from other people's experiences. When my wife and I hired our current accountant to help manage our company's bookkeeping and taxes, we wanted to interview her first. As we walked up to the front door of the accountant's office, my wife paused for a moment and said, *"Sam, don't be impulsive. If I get up to use the restroom, don't sign anything and try not to talk that much. Let's just talk with her and see if she is a good fit for working with us and our company."*

Me (Sam Glenn) - as a young boy eating Peanut Butter

I pretty much look the same today!

When we arrived at the accountant's office for the interview, we sat in a small conference room and chatted about what seemed to be the normal run down of how her services work and the associated costs. It was cut and dry stuff, but then she said something that made her glow in the dark and got our full attention. What she said in that moment separated her from the crowd. She looked at us and spoke with a sense of humbleness and confidence intertwined together, *"Guys, you have to work with someone you feel comfortable with. I have failed at a lot of businesses. I admit it. I have learned some expensive lessons from my failures, which I find valuable to share with my clients, so they don't experience the same things I did or have to endure those expenses. You just happen to be sitting in the office of my most successful business."*

And, that was it. Failing at business or anything for that matter isn't fun. Nobody enjoys losing and it takes a lot to admit your mistakes and be realistic about them. This spoke to us. My wife glanced over at me with a little grin because she knows my story. If there is anyone who knows my true tale of facing fears and failures, it is her. My stories about overcoming goofs have become the cornerstone of my speaking and writing career. I never set out to become a professional speaker or writer, but as I began to share with others the lessons that I learned from my own experiences, I noticed that others felt a sense of positive resonance with their own situations. They were grateful for the information.

Some of the traits of a person with Attention Deficit Disorder (ADD) like me are that we can sometimes miss important information and be overly impulsive in our decision-making process without thinking what the outcome or consequences might be. So, when my wife gives me this reminder pep talk, I don't pout or snap at her, *"I KNOW! GEESSHHH!"* I know it is coming from a place of love to protect us and prevent regretful moments in the future. I welcome this kind of encouragement. I should also point out that we set some healthy boundaries to help me as well. Some of which include me not watching infomercials, the home shopping network, shopping at the dollar store or Wal-Mart when I am tired and finally not visiting the puppy store without my wife's supervision. So far, the boundaries have saved us a lot of money and dysfunctional outcomes.

We respected the humble admission from our new

accountant and were even more delighted to be sitting in the office of her most successful business. We didn't even mind paying the little extra for her services. It is never easy to admit a personal and professional setback, but if you are able to find a way to turn your trials into stepping stones, it can become the most significant experience that you can share and the most encouraging story that others can hear.

Remind yourself
that it's okay not
to be perfect.

Man Down in The Buffet Line...Again!

If I had to pinpoint the exact moment where my life started leaning in a more positive direction, it would have to be an experience that I had in a buffet line. What happened was an accident, but the surveillance footage might suggest otherwise. I joke, of course, but mostly I remember seeing the bacon. In my enthusiastic effort to reach for the bacon, I accidentally bumped into another person. To be truthful, I may have run over another human. I think the NFL and WWE would be impressed with this take down. Fair warning, it is never a great idea to get in the way of a 6'6" and 285-pound man like me, especially in a buffet line.

I looked down at the person who I had just knocked over; then I glanced over at my breakfast plate which now rested on the floor. I may have even debated in my mind who or what to get first. I knew right then that this wasn't going to be an easy-going breakfast for me. There was something a little more unusual waiting for me in that buffet line and luckily this time it wasn't food poisoning. Something was happening. It was something my life desperately needed and something I could not have possibly imagined – it was a date with destiny.

When I share the story of who I knocked over in the buffet line, it often draws surprised looks along with big smiles. At the time, I had no idea of the icon that this person was. I wasn't familiar with his name or work, but some of you reading this will know who he is right away. This man was the legendary Zig Ziglar. At the time, Zig was one of the most prominent motivational speakers and business authors on the planet. I just thought he was someone who happened to have a very unusual name.

After I assisted Mr. Ziglar up from the ground and picked off some of the scrambled eggs I got on his suit coat, I apologized profusely. We chatted for a brief moment as I wanted to be sure that he was okay and not about to call the buffet cops or press charges. He handled the knockdown with a classy attitude. He laughed it off when I told him that this wasn't the first time I had knocked someone over at a buffet. His wife quickly came over to see what happened. Instead of referring to me as the buffet bully, Zig kindly introduced me to his wife Jean Ziglar who he fondly referred to as the Red Head. He introduced me as a motivated and enthusiastic buffet-goer. It got a good laugh. That, my friends, was my introduction to Mr. Zig Ziglar and the first step to moving in a new and more positive direction for my life.

(Now, if you have never heard of Zig Ziglar, take a few minutes to google him, watch some of his videos, and

listen to some of his audios. You will thank me for it. Zig passed in 2012, but his legacy will live on as one of the most influential motivational speakers on the planet. His impact and voice will forever be embedded in time.)

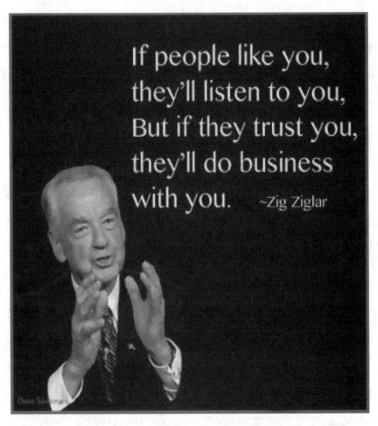

(Here is Zig and one of my favorite quotes of his!)

Meet the Former Me...

Before I finish the story of knocking over Zig Ziglar at the buffet, I need to explain why that was such a noteworthy event for me. At the time of this incident, I wasn't in the most stable place emotionally or physically. I was feeling negative. I was battling depression, feeling defeated in life. It was kindergarten all over again, multiplied by 100. I tried to make sense of things by talking with a counselor. Basically, what I got from her was that my issues had issues. When she told me that, all I could do was wonder if my insurance company would laugh when I asked if my issues qualified for more coverage.

There is absolutely nothing wrong with sitting down with someone who will listen, help you sort out your thoughts and help make some sense of your experiences. In my case, I couldn't afford more than a few sessions, and I was back on my own like a lost puppy.

People always ask me after my speeches: *"Have you always been a positive person?"*

The answer is: *"Nope."* In fact, I have to work on it even more today. Back then, I was scarcely getting by on the lies I told myself and others. The lies were excuses to justify why I was down and why life wasn't unfolding the way I wanted. I blamed others and wasn't ready to take ownership for my choices.

To be more specific, my emotional management skills were a little out of sync. I didn't know how to use my attitude as a force that would work on my behalf. I was functioning in life but with a destructive and defeated attitude. I doubted myself, and I was afraid to try new things. I got lazy, stopped caring, and gave up on myself. You get the picture—my own attitude was tripping me up and preventing me from overcoming setbacks. My greatest disability was my thinking – *"Stinking Thinking"* as Mr. Ziglar referred to it in his speeches. I didn't understand how "attitude" really works; it was just something we have heard about since we were kids. After exploring the subject with a focused effort, I truly "GOT IT." I was superstitious about how things unfolded in life, and I hoped for luck on a daily basis. I didn't attribute any significant role in my life to my attitude. All I knew was that I was unhappy with myself, so I offered free room and board to guilt, resentment and anger. My attitude had become a liability.

You might be thinking, *"Sam, I am not that negative. I have never have been as far into the dark side as you are describing."*

And, I say, *"Super!"* However, if there is anything I have learned, our human attitude is always at work – either working for us or working against us—and we determine the direction it goes every day. You may be a positive person who hits a few mental potholes from time to time. So, perhaps, you do not require a complete attitude overhaul. However, even with your attitude awareness, everyone's attitude requires a little maintenance from time to time to keep going in the direction that works for us.

Attitude maintenance doesn't have to be drudgery or a pain in the bum. It can be quite the opposite. It's not about Peter Pan positivity and thinking happy thoughts when bad things happen. Rather, establishing strength in our attitude works to solve, create, mend, understand, innovate and keep moving forward despite life's unexpected surprises.

Almost 17 years ago, I was lost and overwhelmingly negative. I was scraping by financially working odd jobs delivering newspapers in the early morning hours when most people were still sleeping. Eventually, I got a full time job working the graveyard shift as a janitor and floor cleaner. It was honest hard work but truthfully not my calling. I could never settle into it, because my heart was not in it. Don't get me wrong; I wanted more for myself out of life. But, due to some unfortunate failures, I was feeling alone, afraid and bored with what seemed like minimal options. I didn't know what choice to make next out of fear that it would be the wrong one. The emotions of fear, doubt and negativity taunted me day and night. I didn't know how to silence them. It was becoming evident that something had to change and soon.

Great works are performed, not by strength, but by perseverance."

-Samuel Johnson

A bad
attitude is like a
flat tire. You can't go
anywhere until you
change it.

My Early Morning Chats With Zig Ziglar

"Sometimes we get stink'n think'n and need to take time to do a check up from the neck up."
– Zig Ziglar

Meeting Zig Ziglar was a big highlight for me. Since he was known worldwide and interacted with thousands of new people every year, I was lucky that our encounter ensured he would not forget me. When I learned more about Zig, who he was and what he was about, I reached out to his office to try and connect. This was before social media, so I called up. When his secretary asked if Zig knew me, I laughed and said to mention the guy he met at the buffet. I got an immediate call back. When Zig and I chatted, it was mostly by phone and super early in the morning. It was so early that a few times I was tempted to let the answering machine pick up. Sometimes I wasn't ready to roll out of bed yet. I mean who wants to have deep meaningful talks about success and life at 5:00 A.M.? I would be good to go at 10 A.M., but Zig was up and moving and when Zig calls you better pick up. I had attitude problems, and he had solutions. I would stagger to the phone in the dark of the early morning and try to answer the phone without bed voice, when your mouth is so dry and the first things you say don't sound quite normal or even quite human. You sound like a Sasquatch waking up. My voice requires some warm up time, but I would pick up the phone and act like I had been up for hours living with passion. Zig would ask, *"Did I wake you?"*

"Oh… no, sir. I have been up doing pushups and baking cookies all night. I never go to bed."

I tried to play it off, but Zig knew better and just laughed. Our discussions mostly related to life, attitude and God. Zig was a great man of faith; he wasn't ashamed to share his love for God and God's love for us. I think sometimes I may have perplexed Zig that I was such a slow learner. I didn't know how to embrace the benefits of becoming a positive person. I had trouble transitioning into a student of personal and professional development. It took some time for me to warm up to the idea. I was searching but lazy at the same time. I was looking for the results without doing the work, and it never works in our favor going that route. Zig made an excellent case for the subject of being positive and lived his message as an example to follow. However, I remained skeptical because I felt, that at times even though I would try and be positive, something negative or bad would always happen. So to me, it felt pointless. I thought, *"Why work so hard to be positive when negative stuff is going to happen anyway?"*

It took years to embrace the worth of this life lesson:

A good life lesson: Being positive doesn't stop negative or unexpected things from happening, but choosing a more positive attitude will equip you to deal with the negative stuff better than a negative attitude will.

The benefit of being positive is that it equips us to be resilient, to summon creative solutions and to make firm and proactive choices. Negative thinking promotes the use of negative words, negative thinking and negative actions. Negative thinking closes down the notion that there are any possible options. It pulls you down and it takes others with you. Negative thinking makes unexpected setbacks much worse, and I am speaking from personal experience.

A NEGATIVE
MIND WILL
NEVER
GIVE YOU A
POSITIVE LIFE

I Didn't Want to Embarrass Myself for the World to See

Becoming a professional speaker and author was not in my master plan. I had no desire or ambition for that type of career. In fact, I willingly and happily took F's and zeroes in college for any assignment that required me to give a presentation or speech. It is not something I recommend, but I was just too scared to speak in front of others. I didn't like the feeling of everyone staring at me with my hands sweating, forgetting what I was going to say next and flubbing my words. When I was in front of others, my heart would beat a mile a minute, my hands would shake and I simply looked foolish. It was too nerve-racking so I bowed out of any required presentations to the response of my professors, *"Mr. Glenn, you realize you will get an F on this project if you do not get up and present your material?"*

"I do and am okay with that."

"Mr. Glenn, you want to fail?"

"No, but my fear of fainting or peeing my pants during a speech is greater than my fear of failure."

I actually saw someone faint during a speech once and that pretty much sealed the deal for me: *"I would never speak in front of groups or audiences. No way!"* It's funny how things have changed since then. I never would have imagined that one day I would win awards like **Speaker of the Year** and speak to audiences as large as 75,000 at stadium events. I can only tell you that excitement resides where there once lived fear! I found a way to have fun with my speaking and to make it fun for others. *(More on this story a bit later – you will enjoy it!)*

Everybody Likes a Good Roast ...I Think

In 2002, I was asked to be a closing luncheon speaker for the National Speakers Association in Orlando, Florida. The year before, they had asked me to speak at the same conference to the children of the speakers attending. It was a hoot. These kids' parents were all professional speakers, so the last thing they wanted to hear was another speech. When they introduced me to this room filled with mostly high school kids, they looked bored expecting it to be like mom or dad speaking. No way! I interacted with them, asking them what it was like having parents that speak for a living and doing impersonations of speakers. Let's just say, it wasn't a normal speech and one they had never seen before. They laughed so hard it was insane. I guess word spread about the experience because the next year they asked me to speak to everyone at the conference.

(Here is a picture of Zig and myself after my speech in 2002. I am not sure what I said to make him laugh, but it may have been, "If you don't smile I will knock you over at a buffet again." I don't recall exactly, but it was a good laugh.)

The highlight of that speaking engagement was Zig sitting in the audience and hearing me speak for the first time. I am not sure if it was nerves or the fact that I was talking to a room full of peers, but looking back I think I actually spent more time roasting people in the audience than sharing a well-groomed message. It was honestly pretty fun. To this day, I am not sure why I went that route, but it worked. I mean, who doesn't love a good roast? (And, I am not talking beef here.) That is my unadvertised gift - I have a special talent for roasting people, mostly uptight people. I would make the legendary roaster Don Rickles proud. I don't think I could make a living at it, but it sure is fun to do at times.

When it was all said and done, the experience was a memorable success. Zig waited until everyone had gone and left for the day so we could chat over a cup of coffee for a few minutes. It was a rare honor to have personal time with him. I knew Zig was a busy guy and everyone was always trying to get his attention and a few minutes with him. So, I respected the quality of his time. It wasn't like we talked every day or hung out at buffets or even met up at the Olive Garden on holidays. In fact, the only family member I have met was his wife. His mentorship existed long before I became a full-time professional speaker. He knew I had a fear of public speaking and that I had no desire to be in the spotlight or to pursue such a career. The focus of our conversations revolved around education, faith and personal development. Zig would share his vintage stories and make suggestions that he thought would benefit me. He left it in my hands to act on his shared wisdom.

Every time you are tempted
to react in the same old way, ask
if you want to be a prisoner of
the past or a pioneer of the
future.

Deepak Chopra

Own Your Originality

This might be a good point in the book to draw attention to something else people often wonder and ask me. Since I am a professional speaker like Zig, do I strive to copy or be like Zig? The answer is *"No."* In fact, I have never tried to be like any other speaker "out there" and have no desire to be. My specialty is being the most entertaining and uplifting opening kick-off and closing speaker. That is how everyone knows me. The two most memorable parts of any event are the opening and closing. I like to be either the launching pad or the exclamation point that revs people up to get them started or sends them on their way feeling invigorated to face work and life with a renewed attitude. Either way those are my hot spots and I love filling them.

I have used my originality to build my speaking business to where it is today. And, that is a key **life**

lesson: Use the value of your originality to achieve your dreams. I remember once meeting a relativity new speaker at a banquet dinner and noticed in his presentation that he was trying to be just like Tony Robbins. So, I inquired of him, *"Why not be the best you that you can be? The world already has a Tony Robbins. What the world wants and desires the most is the real you. You are in great demand already and don't even know it. Just be the best you that you can be. Your originality is where your value is. It is what makes you priceless."*

I love what I do, but it came with the price of hard work. In fact, Zig never opened any doors for me other than the ones in my mind. I never asked for a leg up or whether he knew anyone that would want to hire me to speak. Not once did I even consider asking for that. I wanted to build my business on word of mouth. My best marketing is a great speech. Part of my message to organizations, who value customers, is your best marketing is a great experience. Even if the customer has a poor experience with your company and you find a way to turn it around that makes them happy – that is a great experience and it builds loyalty.

Now the ugly truth is that every so often newer speakers who struggle to solidify their originality or branding might copycat or pirate the materials of well-established speakers. This kind of shady behavior eventually comes back to bite them; they lose all credibility. I see this happen enough in this industry to share some solid advice with authority: **Stay original!** Even if it takes you a little longer to figure out what makes you unique and different, stay true to your own stuff and give credit where credit is due. Don't get frustrated if you don't figure it all out in the short time it takes you to drive through a fast food restaurant. Some things require a little more time to be done right and are worth going back to redo over and over again.

As many will attest who have heard me speak, I definitely stay true to my originality. I say this because, even though Zig influenced me a great deal, I have never tried to be him or copy him in anyway. The only things I have copied from Zig are his passion for making a difference and his work ethic in personal and professional development. Zig was generous enough to extend a little of his time to help me improve the quality of my thinking. When I encountered setbacks, I used them as stepping stones to success, rather than rocks in my pockets weighing me down.

Educating
the mind
without
educating the
heart is no
education
at all.
— Aristotle

The only **people** without problems are in cemeteries.

- Dr. Norman Vincent Peale

It Didn't Happen Overnight and Typically Never Does

Unfortunately, even after meeting and getting to know the captain of motivation – Zig Ziglar – my mediocre attitude didn't transform overnight. Zig, as positive and knowledgeable as he was, could not change my average attitude for the better. That part was my job and that is your job. Whatever attitude we choose to have is a personal choice. Nobody can choose your attitude but you. Nobody can change your attitude but you. While it has been close to 20 years since that epic buffet showdown with Zig, I am still working on my attitude. Even as I write this book, I am working on it. I often joke that I have a great attitude but other people keep messing it up! Do you ever feel like that at times? There is an amazing quotation from the late Victor Frankl, *"When we are no longer able to change a situation, we are challenged to change ourselves."* It was obvious that what I was doing wasn't working. I think we all get a little caught up in that process of doing the same thing over and over again and expecting a new result (some people call this insanity). It's like putting money in a slot machine, hoping with each pull that you hit the big winner. But, in the end, the house always gets your money. **A good life lesson: We can't expect others to change us or expect new results with attitudes and actions that don't work. We have to be willing to change ourselves and go from there.**

For the past 17 years, I have dedicated myself to studying the human attitude and the extent of how it works for us or against us. In the pursuit of what is worthwhile to us, I now realize that we all face burn-out and mental exhaustion from time to time. I know I have on many occasions. The positive spark of motivation that revs our engine needs a little maintenance service. Our attitude needs servicing just like our automobile, but, in this case, we are the technicians. Maybe you have experienced that – you get drained from all of life's detours and feel downright fatigued. You are holding on to that last fiber of hope, but you are just too tired to keep moving forward. You begin to question what's possible, *"Why does everything have to be so hard?"* Or, maybe others have let you down. They said one thing and did another and it created an inconvenient detour for you. The road of life is filled with detours.

EVERY FAILURE, FLOP AND FEAR CAN BECOME A STEP
TO YOUR DREAM

Not All Change is Bad

Sometimes things don't always go according to plan. If you ever watch future hall of fame quarterback Peyton Manning run his offensive plays, you will see that he changes plans at the last second. In the huddle, the offense meets and Peyton gives them the planned play. However, in football there is something called an audible call. This is where the QB examines the defensive line up and calls a different play at the line of scrimmage. The offense is always aware that plans can change at any moment and that they need to be ready for it. When Peyton calls a change of plays, he is doing it so his team can make a better play. Sometimes, you have to abandon the original plans and go with newer ones that will work most in your favor.

This happens in life too, but we don't always call an audible. Life does it for us. Have you ever had big plans to head in one direction in life and ended up somewhere completely different because of an unexpected detour? But, in the long run, it turned out to be the greatest piece of good fortune? You found a way for yourself and your dream. You found a way to make something work when it seemed that there was literally no way.

To underline what it means to find a way when life gives us a detour, here is a story about a little boy who set out with the determination to achieve one thing. When it didn't work out, he found a new and rewarding route. I am sure you have heard this story; it's a favorite. As the story goes, a little boy was overheard talking to himself as he strutted through the backyard, wearing his baseball cap and toting a ball and bat. *"I'm the greatest hitter in the world,"* he announced. Then he tossed the ball into the air, swung at it, and missed. *"Strike One!"* he yelled. Undaunted, he picked up the ball and said again, *"I'm the greatest hitter in the world!"* He tossed the ball into the air. When it came down, he swung again and missed. *"Strike Two!"* he cried.

The boy then paused a moment to examine his bat and ball carefully. He spit on his hands and rubbed them together. He straightened his cap and said once more,

"I'm the greatest hitter in the world!" Again he tossed the ball up in the air and swung at it. He missed. *"Strike Three!"* the boy exclaimed.

He thought for a minute, smiled big and exclaimed with pure enthusiasm, *"I'm the greatest pitcher in the world!"*

Sometimes things don't always work out according to our plans and we have to rethink our strategies, beliefs and do a gut check, *"Do I give in and give up, or get up and make a way?"*

If It Seems Like There Is No Way, Then It is Up To You to Make One

When it seems like there are no more options left and you have run out of runway, you have to make a choice to give up or make a way. Making a way for yourself is about "YOU" not giving up on yourself, especially in those questionable moments when there are only fumes left in your emotional and physical tank that barely keep you going. You probably have seen the movie "Rudy," the real life story of Daniel "Rudy" Ruettiger and his determination to play football at the University of Notre Dame. He had to overcome a mountain of challenges and setbacks to achieve his tall dream, a dream that seemed almost impossible. When Rudy tried to pitch the film idea about his story to Hollywood, it was rejected several times because they felt it would not be a hit movie. Rudy's response to them was that more people will be able to relate to an underdog than to a superhero. It is a story of hope – the power of a dream.

The movie gives me goose bumps every time I see it. Rudy was right; more people do relate and root for the underdog. I remember walking through the mall one day and they started to play the movie on the TV's that were for sale in Radio Shack. I stepped in to watch just a little and ended up standing there for the entire movie, even though I had already seen it at least five times. We imagine it is us overcoming the odds. We want that that feeling. We want to experience it in our everyday reality.

Rudy faced one detour after another, but he found the spirit and willingness to get up and keep moving forward. He found his way. Life's challenges will attempt to deceive you into believing you have come to a dead end and that nothing else will work. This is why I love history which is filled with substantial evidence that there is a way. History is filled with people like you and me who demonstrated that when it <u>looks like</u> there is no way, we can keep looking and <u>make</u> a way.

NEVER LET SUCCESS GET TO YOUR HEAD. NEVER LET FAILURE GET TO YOUR HEART.

Adversity is a Royal Pain in the Attitude

Let's be real, life is filled with unexpected detours and bumps in the road. They are inconvenient, uncomfortable and a pain in the butt. Yet, if you have the right kind of thinking, positive and resilient, you will find a way to get to where you want to go.

My mom once told me that adversity touches us all at some point and we never know exactly when or in what form it will take. It just shows up without an invitation. Adversity can be likened to an irritating, unpleasant and unannounced guest who shows up and attempts to make your life a living nightmare. Without permission, it attacks our attitude and invades our emotions with stress, frustration, confusion, depression, doubt and fear.

The late Norman Vincent Peale stated it well, *"The only people without problems can be found in a cemetery."* As long as you have air pumping through your lungs, you will face adversity.

Adversity has an agenda to make us to feel like failures similar to that playground bully who makes us cry. While adversity is inevitable, how we handle it is our choice. Surprisingly, it can be your ultimate stepping stone and boost to your desired success. Adversity makes us want to crumble, cry and yell at the top of our lungs when things don't work out. That is normal and human. It's OK to have those emotions, but don't be tricked into a hasty response. What I mean is don't react out of fear or anger. It will only lead to more turmoil.

In the face of my own setbacks and failures, it felt like a 100 pound weight was pulling me down physically and emotionally. Over the years, I have heard numerous stories of how the ugly side of adversity has tried to steal people's dreams and leave their life in ruins – the stories of the wife who lost her husband in an accident; the marriage that failed; the rebellious teenager running with the wrong crowd, the financial ruin of a lost business, the layoff; the foreclosure, the sexual abuse;

the eating disorder; the storm that destroyed everything, etc…

I don't know what your story is, but a **good life lesson is: We all face personal storms and setbacks, and the key to finding the strength to keep moving forward is the strength we find in each other.**

"Even a mistake may turn out to be the one thing necessary to a worthwhile achievement."

- Henry Ford

How to Flush A
Business Down The Drain

When I was in college, I took ownership of a company my grandfather, Richard Albertson, had built and run for more than 30 years. It was his passion and he would use the profits to give to his kids and grandkids and create experiences and positive memories.

Near the time of his death, he entrusted this business to our family. When he was sick with lung cancer, my mom packed up her three boys and headed seven hours from Plainfield, Illinois, to Marine, Minnesota to help Gramps keep the business running. Looking back on his system of work, it was hard work and left us with lots of blisters on our hands. It was also dangerous work if you didn't pay attention. Grandpa manufactured wild bird products – raw nesting materials packaged with a metal dispenser to hold the nesting materials. You may chuckle a little, but it was a unique item that sold extremely well for more than 30 years, along with other wild bird products like birdseed and bird houses. Here is something you may not know. Gardening has become the number one hobby in America, and the second largest hobby is birding. Bet you didn't know that! I sure didn't when we took over grandpa's business.

So, Gramps had a good thing going! I was still in high school when we helped him in his shop. He didn't have much strength to do the manual labor, so we had to lend our muscles to assist with that part. We had to chop up the nesting materials (fibers, rope, yarns) by hand. There was a huge stump log and a sharp ax. That's how we cut it, and it had to be a specific length. Even with gloves, I had blisters after 10 minutes. After 20 minutes, I admitted that I was truly a wimp. Then, we had to use a lathe that would spin and coil this heavy duty metal into a dispenser to hold the nesting materials. You had to be very careful, because if you got your hand caught while the lathe was spinning… well, it's not a picture that I want to paint for you. It was very difficult work, and you could not lose focus for one second or you would get hurt. There were about 20 plus steps from concept to completion. I remember wondering how Grandpa did this by himself for so long. He didn't get rich doing it, but he was able to help others out. As I mentioned earlier, he created experiences and memories that still remain fresh in my mind over 30 years later. Grandpa loved his family and he worked hard to make sure you felt special and loved.

When Grandpa got close to the end of his life, he felt comfortable handing over his 30-year-old business to us, because we showed him that we could do the work. Some family members were not happy that it was given to just us, but we were the only ones that showed up when he asked for help and I don't think they understood what the work truly entailed. It wasn't fun work by any means. Our family was also going through some financial hardships and grandpa gave us something that helped us out. It helped where and when we needed it.

Grandpa passed on and we tried to make him proud by working hard to keep his business going. A few years passed, and I began to see a much larger picture for my Grandpa's business. I don't fully recall the details of how I ended up taking over things, but I did. I had no business experience, but I wanted to show everyone the potential that it had. I worked around the clock to keep things going. However, I faced many little setbacks. I trusted unethical people by giving money to those who said they could help me achieve success with my grandpa's business but delivered only empty promises. Looking back, I honestly think I would have gotten a better return on my money if I had flushed it down the toilet. That's how unethical these people were. People would dangle that perpetual carrot (what I wanted to achieve in business and in life) in front of my face and I could never get it because they kept pulling it away. I would continue to dish out more and more time and money in hopes that I could take my grandpa's business to a new level. I borrowed and maxed out every credit card to keep operations going. Little did I know, I was about to encounter a very difficult detour.

Our Choices Are What Write Our Stories

It was hard to sleep. I kept tossing and turning. My mind would not shut off. It kept going from one thought to another. I rolled over to see the time on the clock and it was almost 2A.M.. I let out a big sigh and took a deep breath. With everything I had left in me, I sat up and put my feet on the ground. I rubbed my eyes, hoping that I was in a dream. The reality of my life at this very moment was that I was flat broke, heavily in debt, and sleeping on borrowed floor space in my mom's apartment. To earn money, I delivered newspapers at 2 A.M. three nights a week. I eventually found a job working nights as a janitor. There is nothing wrong with either job as it was honest pay for hard work, but I didn't see it as my calling. I was humbled and developed a deeper appreciation for those who do work really hard to provide for their families by meeting their needs through such vocations.

I felt depressed and I could not regain any sense of ambition. I carried a backpack of guilt about how I had let so many people down. The more I thought about it, the more depressed I became. My mind would drift in and out of reality wondering how things had gone so wrong.

Do the Math...
No Brakes + Bad Attitude =
No Good

*"I have some really good news and some bad news.
First the bad news -- the brakes stopped working 2 miles
ago. The really good news is I no longer need to pee! "*

The laundry list of things going wrong kept growing. It was around 3 A.M. when the brakes on my car went out. I was coming up to a major intersection, the light was red, but the car was not stopping. I knew the car needed new brakes, but I had no idea the situation was this bad. All the brake fluid leaked out. So, I had no brakes! I started pumping the brakes like a madman, but it didn't work. I even yelled *"Stoooooppppp!!"* several times, but that didn't work either. My car was on its own, and I truly was the passenger sitting in the driver's seat. As the car coasted forward, I heard what sounded like a 12-year-old girl screaming at the top of her lungs, but I realized shamefully it was just me screaming.

I actually saw my life flash before me. I thought I was dead meat for sure. I pictured myself showing up at the Pearly Gates and St. Peter asking me,

"Hey! How did you get here?"

"Ummm... I just drove here... literally."

My car glided right through one of the busiest intersections in Naperville, Illinois. The light was red and I went right through it. I remember taking a deep breath and holding it, my heart pounding as I quickly looked all over for other car lights to see if someone would hit me or I them. By a miracle, and I do mean it was a miracle, there were no cars at that intersection. My car kept going and in front of me was a Phillips 66 gas station. It was my only option to stop the car. I saw the 8 to 10 inch curb in front of the gas station and thought if I can steer the car into it, I can stop. I didn't have time to weigh my options, so I went with my gut. I knew it wouldn't be pretty, but at least it would end the joy ride.

I hit the curb – HARD! I hit it harder than I had expected and my car flew right over it into a patch of grass. Like a scene out of Willie Wonka, when everyone was screaming to stop the terrifying boat ride, I came to an abrupt halt. I let out the big breath of air I had been holding in. It was a miracle that I didn't hit anyone and nobody hit me. Whewwww....what a ride!

The guy working the graveyard shift at the gas station came scrambling out from behind the register, yelling in a panic, *"You okay man?! Something bit you? You drunk? What's wrong with you?!"*

"I am okay. My brakes crapped out!"

"Crapped out?! I would say by the way you drove up, those brakes are just crap. Young man, it's a good

thing there weren't any cars around. You sure got lucky. I saw you drive right through that red light and the way you were driving towards our station, I thought you were going to end up on top of our register. By the way, there is a restroom around the corner. You kinda look like you might need one."

That guy was right. I did have to use the bathroom. When I looked the car over, I had no idea how I was going to pay to fix the damage. I mean, I hardly had enough to pay for gas, much less fix the brakes and the damages. It was pretty much what I call burnt toast – it was done.

Dude, Wake UP!
This isn't a Prank Phone
Call!!! I Need Help!

The gas station guy was nice enough to let me use the phone to call someone to come get me. I didn't know who to call at first. It was 3 A.M.. Who was going to pick me up? My brother Ben lived about 20 minutes away, so I tried him first. We didn't have cell phones back then. Well, actually we did. It was a big brick phone and it cost about the same amount to make a 5-minute call as it did to fill your gas tank. It was crazy expensive with bad reception.

I got lucky again, Ben picked up. I wasn't sure he would, since over the years I had a habit of prank calling his house at weird hours of the night. It's just something we did to joke with each other.

"Ben! It's Sam. Dude, this isn't a prank phone call! I need your help! The brakes went out on the car. I crashed into a gas station and I need to finish my paper route. Can you please come get me and help me out?"

Ben, sounding barely awake, agreed to get me. Now, the pressure was on. If I was going to get paid, I had to get all those newspapers delivered before sunrise.

When Ben pulled up, I thought he was going to be in a cranky mood for waking him up, but he was really cool about the whole situation. Maybe he was nice because he was the one who sold me the car that just traumatized me. I didn't pay much for it, but almost paid for it with my life. Ben was a champion that night. Since my attitude was in the dumps already, he made the rest of the night and the situation tolerable. I was tired and just wanted to go back to bed. The weight of all my worries was exhausting. But, surprisingly, that night Ben and I shared in a few laughs. That laughter helped. Laughing made me not feel so bad about everything. It relaxed me (just like a great peanut butter sandwich). It made me not feel so worried or dwell on everything that was wrong with my life. It made me feel a spark of energy.

Who knows, we may have been slap happy, but it

helped us focus on getting the job done instead of complaining or whining about the situation. We got the job done before the sun came up and I got paid. That is the good news. But, the fact still remained –I didn't have a car anymore.

Do you ever replay things over and over in your mind so much you have dreams about it when you sleep? I just kept replaying over and over that I was a failure and that life was unfair. I was a good person and a hard worker, so why was all this crazy stuff happening? And that's the thing about adversity; it does not discriminate - ever. We are all subject to its consequences. It just felt like I was swinging from one failure to another. After graduating from college with a degree in hand, I was fired from my first two jobs. The newspaper delivery job came after I was fired twice.

Time

has a wonderful way

of showing us

what really matters. :)

I Got Fired Twice Out of the Gate

Before I delivered newspapers and worked nights as a janitor, I had a few other jobs right out of college that didn't quite work out as planned. The first job I had out of the college starting gate was actually working for my brother Ben. He was developing his professional speaking career and I would help by driving him to his speaking engagements and doing whatever else I could to help him. We shared an apartment in Rockville, Indiana, the covered bridge capital of the world. We both thought our apartment, which was the top floor of a very old home, may have been haunted. In addition to living in an old and scary apartment, we both were pretty messy. On one occasion, people stopped by and our place was so messy that we acted like we had just been robbed and the burglars had turned everything over. The truth was that nothing was missing - except our cleaning habits.

Ben was mostly invited to speak at church functions. He took over a ministry called Living Art Ministries for a friend and mentor, Bill Leach. It was a chalk art ministry and Bill would draw the most amazing pictures and share a message with it. When Bill got sick and was no longer healthy enough to travel and fulfill his speaking engagements, he asked if Ben would take over for him. So, Bill generously gave his ministry and his car to Ben (the one with the brakes that went out while I delivered newspapers). Ben used his art background and learned to do chalk art presentations like Bill's.

Many of the churches would have Ben drive up to 300 miles just one way to speak and they would pay Ben in the form of a love offering. After Ben did his chalk talk, the pastor of the church would pass around a plate or basket and whatever people donated was the love offering. It would cost Ben hundreds of dollars in gas, food and lodging on many occasions, and there was no of knowing what the love offering gift would be. So, Ben would travel from one place to another on pure faith. At times, the love offerings would be far less than the travel costs. I always thought that part of the gig was disheartening. We drove a long way for one particular church function. Ben did such a great job and it was evident in the responses and feedback. One lady walked up and told Ben she put $1000 in the love offering for his ministry. I remember seeing Ben just glow when he heard that. That was a lot of money; it would help keep his ministry going for some time. It was a major blessing. However, when the pastor gave Ben the envelope with the love offering gift, there was less than $200 inside. You do the math. Ben inquired about the discrepancy and the pastor of this church said, *"We have never paid any speaker more than $200 and will not pay you more than that."*

The pastor pocketed the balance of the money. That blew me away. It was eye-opening to witness that kind of deceit. The church should be an example of what it means to be a blessing. That incident was not an isolated one. It happened over and over and in different ways. Sometimes, it felt surreal. I couldn't believe people who were in such prominent roles would act in such a way. It was like watching someone stomp out the light of a candle.

Despite these unexpected setbacks, Ben held firm to a resilient attitude. Sometimes he would look visibly disappointed and drained on our long drives home. He would just kind of stare out the window and sit in silence for quite a bit. Usually a pit stop, a bag of Chex mix and a coke would get him back to himself again.

I was still running my grandpa's business while working for Ben. Whatever money I earned working for Ben, which wasn't much, I would pour right back into my grandpa's business to keep it going. I had managed to get a relatively good system in place where I would ship the components of my products to a warehouse in Chicago and they would assemble, store and ship everything from their location. All I had to do was fax any purchase orders to them and they would handle the details of everything else. My vision for Grandpa's company was a tall order on my dream board, but I saw a lot of potential for expansion and growth. However, the lofty vision I had for growth didn't come cheap. As the saying goes, there were always more month left over than there was money. I was learning how to be an entrepreneur and my learning curve was expensive. I went back into the business. I was just waiting for it to take off in a big way.

Trying Something New

While still working or pretending to work for Ben, I suggested we should look into studying Improv at the famous Second City in Chicago. It was nearly four hours away from us -one way- and not budget friendly to what we had in available cash. I don't remember how we did it, but Ben and I found a way to pay for the classes. So, we grabbed a bag of chips, soda and loose change for tolls and headed out on the 4-hour drive up to Chicago. Classes lasted a few hours and so instead of grabbing a beer or food with our classmates, we got in the car and drove four hours home. I won't lie, those were long and exhausting days, but it was an educational experience that still serves both Ben and I today. What we learned there has paid dividends in our professional speaking careers. Our return on investment has been well over a thousand fold and that is being conservative. It taught us better communication, teamwork, creativity, how to think on our feet and how to handle the unexpected in a positive way.

When Ben got married, there just wasn't enough income coming in to keep me on his staff and I was all of his staff. We both moved back to Chicago and set off on our own paths. However, moving proved to be another entertaining experience. It was my job to drive the pickup truck with all our stuff back to Chicago. Have you ever noticed that when you move, it seems like you have ten times more stuff than when you moved in? I am just going to say this in the best way possible, Ben and I had so much crap that it was ridiculous. We didn't have money to pay movers and we only had pickup truck, sold to us by the devil himself, that only worked part of the time. I am not kidding. That truck had a mind of its own. Sometimes it would just accelerate for no reason, turn off for no reason and slow down for no reason. I can't tell you how many mechanics worked on that truck and said, *"This is a weird truck. We can't figure it out."*

Yeah, it was weird. It got weirder when we chose to put our trust in it to move all our lifelong belongings back to Chicago. Since there was not a lot of room on the bed of the truck, we did what they do in New York City. When there is no more room to build outward, you build upwards. We had a tower of junk piled high on the back of that truck. It was so ridiculous looking, it became an attraction for all the neighbors. People were asking, *"Are you just trying to see how high you can pile your stuff?"*

I wish I had the real picture to show you, but it was insane. We used every bungee cord in the tri-county area to tie everything down. Then it was time. It was the moment of truth. I drove the truck a block to see if it would be okay and Ben confirmed, *"Yeah... looks good. Just don't take any corners really sharp and you should be OK."*

Ben was going in a different direction that day, so I was on my own with this tower of stuff. As I drove through the town of Rockville, it was funny watching all the double takes. I even saw one old guy shake his head back and forth like he was saying, *"There goes one crazy human."*

It was crazy. I couldn't believe I agreed to drive that thing 200 miles. I was on the road for close to 20 minutes when it started to rain. It was a light drizzle that gradually grew into a full on raging thunderstorm. I could barely see the road and oddly enough, I started laughing hysterically, because we put Ben's mattress and all his stuff near the top. It got drenched. Ben gave me good advice not to take corners too fast, but he didn't say anything about sharp twists in the road. Well, due to poor visibility caused by the thunderstorm, a sharp twist in the road snuck up on me. When I made it without flying off the road, I was happy. However, the truck felt a lot lighter, I mean, considerably lighter. I had the mirrors on the outside of the truck adjusted in a way so that I could see the mountain of our stuff in the back. When I looked to check on our stuff, the mountain of stuff was gone. GONE! Apparently, when I hit that twist in the road, everything flew off. I couldn't tell at first because of the storm. I pulled over to examine the situation and there was about a good 65% of our stuff in the ditch. There is no way I could pick up all of that myself and redo what we had done. I didn't have a cell phone and so as I was standing there getting drenched from the pouring rain. I started praying for a sign to let it go or to find help. I got my sign in the most significant way. As I slowly walked down into the ditch area to examine the debris of our stuff everywhere, I heard some barking of dogs.

THIS ISN'T GOING TO END WELL FOR ANYONE

The barks got louder and louder as they got closer and closer. When I spotted them, they didn't look friendly or like they wanted to snuggle or lick my face. They were farm dogs who looked like they hadn't eaten in days. The way they were coming at me, I could see it in their eyes – they wanted to use me as a chew toy. I used my gazelle like reflexes and hauled butt back to the truck. That was all the sign I needed and off I went to Chicago. The rest of the trip was uneventful and peaceful, until I got to Ben's new apartment with most of his stuff missing. I don't remember what I told him, I think it was something like, *"I got robbed and the robbers wanted your mattress. Don't ask me why, but they just wanted your stuff, man!"*

When I got settled back in Chicago, I was still ambitious enough to keep my grandpa's business going. I found a job in sales and it was a straight commission sales position. The only experience I gained working there was how to deal with debt because I made zero sales. The company let you to take a draw or allowance against any future earnings, so I did just that. I was getting so far behind and so freaked out that one day, I actually sold my truck during my lunch break. I was tired of it breaking down all the time and a little scared that I was going into debt working 80 hours a week. When the tow truck guy starts becoming a really good friend, I figured it was time to get rid of that ride. I sold it really cheap. It was worth about $3500 plus. I met an interested buyer in the parking lot, and we made a deal for less than half that amount. All I knew was that I had cash in hand and said, *"Wow, so this is what it feels like to hold money."*

When I walked back into the office and sat down at my desk, I said with excitement to everyone in the office, *"Good news, I just made my first sale –I sold my truck!"*

My boss gave me that dumbfounded look, *"Sam, how do you plan on getting home tonight and how are you going to go out on sales calls?"*

My response, *"You know, I didn't really think about that."*

I really didn't think it all the way through. Now, the panic set in. How was I going to get home? What was I going to do for transportation? It is no exaggeration when I tell you; it was pretty embarrassing to have my mom leave her work to come pick me up from my job. She was not happy with me. She drove me to and from work every day until I was able to get another car. But, it wasn't just a relaxed drive to and from work. This was the consequence of my stupidity: my mother lecturing her 26-year-old son for the entire trip to work and all the way home. I was ready to hitch a ride on a pogo stick to work at this point.

Mom was right with her heartfelt words, *"Sam, you need to get your head out of your rear. You need to think and start making some better choices. Stop making choices that keep making your life difficult."*

To say the least, this sales job was NOT a good fit for me or for them. I left that job. A better way of putting it was: I was released, fired, let go, canned, escorted out the door. They gave me an envelope on my way out the door with an invoice to pay back all the money I borrowed against my future sales that I never made. It took me years to pay this back, but eventually when I got on the right track I did – every penny. Even when I was cash poor, I would send something once a month to show good faith in repaying back the debt. Sometimes I would send only $5. I wasn't doing that to be a jerk. I was doing it to communicate that as long as it takes, I would repay the debt. Even when the business went under, I still sent checks to the former owner. I think he appreciated my integrity and I am sure it helped him in his own hard times.

IF WE WAIT UNTIL WE'RE READY, WE'LL BE WAITING FOR THE REST OF OUR LIVES.

Beware of Unethical People And Never be Afraid to Walk or Ask Them to Walk

DON'T LET NEGATIVE THOUGHTS LIVE IN YOUR MIND RENT FREE. KICK THEM OUT!

The pressure and fear of my situation became like a school yard bully. I felt forced into making choices that were not well thought out or in my own best interest. I wasn't using common sense. I took these odd jobs to help sustain my grandfather's business. If I had been smart and took things in small steps, I could have made a very good living and built some savings like my grandfather did for 30 years. As it turns out, I was blinded by my ambition and desire to have it all at once. I lacked patience and I was greedy. I treated my situation like a round of poker – all or nothing. In the end, looking back, all I was doing was throwing money away.

When unethical people know your situation and your motivations to do whatever it takes to make something work, as in my case, they can manipulate you in just about any way they want. They know how to use words and dangle exactly what you want close enough in front of you to get you to believe that if you just hang in there a little longer and keep paying them, it will all work out. One guy, who for the sake of this book I will name Mitch, was helping expand my business and made me promises that would realize my goals for my grandpa's business. As it turns out, he was a wolf in sheep's clothing. He was as unethical as they come. He milked me for just about everything I had earned. I just kept giving him money upon request, and he just took and took and had no shame or moral compass with his actions. The last straw was when I gave him the last $300 I had. When I say it was the last, I counted out pennies to get it to $300. Yes, pennies.

Mitch had his own line of products and he was in Chicago, showcasing his items at a national trade show. I paid thousands to have him and his teams to showcase my item at their booth. He called me near the last day of the trade show and requested $300 for a limousine service. The way he worded it: if they showed up in style in a limousine, then people would buy more. I bought the lie hook line and sinker. Since I had never been in a limo other than my high school prom, I told him I would like to meet them at their hotel and ride with them to the trade show. In response, Mitch tried every which way to talk me out of coming to the trade show.

"Sam, we have it all taken care of. There is no need for you to come into the city and waste your money. Just let us do what we do."

It was the last day of a five-day trade show. I insisted that I wanted to explore, see what other products were being displayed and to learn more about the industry. He called me back two more times to mention a change of plans in an effort to distract me from coming. At this point, I started to think something wasn't right. He left a message on my answering machine that his wife was sick and that they didn't want to get me sick. When I called his hotel and could not reach him, I called his office back in Arizona where he checked his messages frequently. The phone line rang once and his wife picked up. She wasn't even in Chicago. I didn't say anything to her and hung up really fast. I stood up at attention and my eyes got big. Something was up and it was time to follow the fishy smell.

I took the train into Chicago and walked seven blocks to Mitch's hotel. I tried to not disclose my emotions or feelings that something wasn't quite right. When the limousine showed up, it wasn't anything special. The limo ride was less than 10-minutes from the hotel to Chicago McCormack Place. It hardly seemed worth $300, which I later found out was only $50. It was the last day of the trade show and the only day they took a limo. Looking back, I think they just wanted more money and looked for every way for me to pay for their expenses in Chicago. I had already paid their invoice for their hotel, flights and food for the entire week.

When we pulled up, I was expecting something dazzling and grand like a red carpet experience. It wasn't like that at all. We got dropped off near the parking garage. The only person there to see us was a homeless person asking for money. My excitement for the moment melted into steam. My breathing got deeper and my heart pounded in a way I had never experienced.

When I walked on the trade show floor, I was eager to see how my product was being showcased for people to see. I could hardly wait to get to the exhibit booth. I was envisioning something that would soothe my frustrations at being swindled into paying for everything. When I finally reached the exhibit, it was one of the biggest and best. I paid a significant amount to co-exhibit with this guy, but later found out that I had actually paid for it all. His job was to sell my product to distributors and stores all over the world – or so that was the idea he sold me on.

When I walked up to observe his giant booth, I

didn't see my product anywhere. I felt like a kid looking for eggs on an Easter egg hunt. There was nothing to indicate that it even had a place in the exhibit. It was all this guy's product laid out and set up to sell. So I asked, *"Where is my stuff? Why is it not out?"*

Mitch's response, *"Ohh.... Someone must have taken it down or moved it."*

He and his crew of sales people quickly scrambled through boxes of trash in the back to find my stuff. And, like magic they pulled out the little box that I had mailed to them prior to the trade show. The box was filled with all my sample products for the show. It hadn't even been opened. Now, I understood why Mitch was so insistent on trying to get me from coming to the trade show. I wasn't paying him to sell and promote my stuff. It was a smokescreen. I was paying him so he could grow his business and promote his stuff. And, like that, I finally got it.

I didn't say anything, turned and walked along the trade show floor to the exit. I was steaming with anger. I was an easy target. I was gullible with no experience in business. This was the first of several hard and painful lessons to come. When I got home, I called his office and got his answering machine. I left a very calm and stern message.

"Mitch, I will no longer be doing business with you, sending you any more money or having anything to do with you. You are deceptive and unethical, and I want no more part in that."

I was in the bathroom when he called a few days later. He said that if I fired him I would be in violation of our agreement and he would sue me for everything I had.

I called back and again very calmly said, *"I sleep on my mom's living room floor. I have no money left and you already got it all. Do what you need to do, but I promise it will cost you more to sue me than it will cost me. Good luck."*

And, that was it. I never heard from the guy again. It was a hard and expensive lesson that taught me to develop a better future with whom I associate or do business. Years later, I got word that karma eventually caught up with this guy and his life ended up in utter ruins. I am not going to elaborate on how, but it wasn't pretty. It was sad and I am not happy about that because I never wish for bad things to happen to anyone. The lesson is when you do the wrong thing there are consequences to pay. When you make the wrong choices, even though you know what the right thing to do is, you end up hurting yourself in ways that you can't even imagine. It will bite you so hard that you will wish upon a star you could go back in time and do it right. If you know what the right thing to do is, then do it. Anything outside of that won't be pretty.

Hello???
Anyone There??

It was around the first of July in 1996 and I had orders to ship out. However, when I called the warehouse to provide them with the shipping addresses, nobody was picking up. The phone would just ring and ring. There was no answering machine either. I called all day long and every day for a week, until finally someone picked up. It was a woman I had never talked to before and I asked if everything was okay. I had been trying for a week to get a hold of someone. Very calmly, she began to explain to me what happened. *"Mr. Glenn, I apologize, but the warehouse that stored and packaged your products had a fire and everything was lost in the fire."*

Looking back, my response was not very well

thought out. I said to this woman, *"Even my stuff ?!"*

"Yes, Sam, it's all gone."

"How did the fire start?"

"They think it was electrical."

"So what should I do now?"

"Sam, I don't know. Did you insure everything?"

"No, was I supposed to? Nobody told me I had to?"

"I guess you will have to figure things out."

When I hung up the phone, my eyes were glazed from disbelief. I sat in silence and shock for what seemed like almost an hour. I gave everything I had, every penny I had, and just like that it was gone. GONE! There were no resources or time to recover and start over. I had purchase orders on my desk and no product or money to buy new materials to start over. I imported I w specific items from around the world and subcontracted with the people who ran the warehouse that burned down. So, Gramp's business of 30 years was done. And, just like that, I was broke and in some serious debt. Not only was I working to keep the company running, I borrowed from everyone with the promise of a substantial return. I made the promise of a good return based on raw ambition and uncalculated expectations. It was foolish. Now, I had no way of paying anyone back. I was broke; in shock, and draining any positivity I had left working in me.

I remember thinking, *"What do I tell my mom?"* Mom had entrusted everything from her father's business to me. It was a big responsibility and she would frequently check in on me to see how it was all going. She was happy that I had a vision, passion and enthusiasm for Grandpa's business, but she always warned me to be smart and take things one step at a time. I let my ego get in the way and didn't listen to any sound advice from anyone. I tried to do it my own way and I had put my trust in unethical people who didn't really have my best interest at hand.

I don't remember how I told Mom or anyone else for that matter. I think when I asked Mom if I could move in with her for a while and sleep on the living room floor, she got the idea that something wasn't right. Plus creditors where tracking me down and kept calling her house. I had to come clean and admit my failure. I was sick from it.

The shock of what happened eventually wore off. Then it hit me and hit me hard, the reality of having nothing, feeling like nothing and having nothing to start over with. I put my head into the palms of my hands and cried. Apparently, I can cry pretty loud because I made everyone in McDonald's feel slightly uncomfortable. McDonald's asked me to leave so I wouldn't scare anymore customers into thinking I was crying over bad food.

I felt like such a loser. I had no money, no job, nothing. I started taking money from my mom's money jar to buy lottery tickets in hopes that I would win all my money back and pay everyone I owed and start over. No winning tickets. I wanted to wish it all away, but it wasn't that simple. I was responsible for my choices and there are consequences to our choices. Apologizing to those I let down didn't seem like a big enough action to clean up the mess I had created.

My Walk of Shame

I was in such a huge financial predicament. I had borrowed a great deal of money from a lot of people. I had maxed out my brother Chris's credit cards to the sum of over $23,000 with an interest rate of almost 24%. I literally destroyed my brother's credit when he was about to get married. One guy gave me his granddaughter's college funds in hopes of a big return to give to her at a later time. My college roommate trusted me with his money. Others helped co- sign for large loans. I maxed out all of my personal credit. I was advised to declare bankruptcy, the last resort on my list of options. I tried to find any other solution, but the fear and pressure were so much that I did what I didn't want to. My shame and depression multiplied.

My feet felt like cement bricks as I got out of my car and walked up to the courthouse to file bankruptcy. I had to wait in a hallway with a lot of people who were also waiting to file for bankruptcy. Not a single happy face there; it was the walk of shame for most. Some dazed looks echoed, *"How did this happen?"*

"Mr. Glenn? Sam Glenn?" "Yes."

"It's your turn; please come in."

I was escorted into a small, poorly lit cold room. I sat down at a table with a voice recorder propped in front of me. What they do is read out each debt you have, and you have to verbally verify that is in fact your debt. With each debt being read off, all I could really hear was the echo of my inner voice saying, *"I failed. You're a failure. Sam, you will never amount to anything great. Give up."*

My shoulders sunk as low as they could go as they finished reading of each of my debts. I stood and walked out of that room in a very solemn shuffle. Every eye in the hallway was fixed on me as they knew exactly what had just happened. That hallway walk was like the movie *Dead Man Walking*. It was a walk of shame to my car that, even though it was only 100 yards, seemed like a mile long. I could feel every blink of my eyelids as sweat ran down my face and I tried to hold back tears. I felt as though my car keys weighed a ton, and so I just sat there to decompress a little before I took off.

I might point out that I didn't submit all of my debts to the bankruptcy court. I stepped it up and I worked to pay off the grandfather who invested his granddaughter's college money with a little extra. I paid off several personal loans as well. In fact, for almost two years, I paid one guy 20 bucks a month to show good faith. It showed I was committed to integrity. He was quite surprised when he got his final payment, after I started having some success, in one big lump sum. It was good to get that weight off my back. Debt is not fun to have. And, if you do have debt, you have to get smart about it or it will really weigh you down. I am a huge fan of David Ramsey's material on financial fitness and dealing with debts. If you struggle with managing your money or just need some solid perspective on whatever your situation is, David's stuff is as good as it comes. He has helped millions of people. I am a fan!

Experience is not what happens to a man. It is what a man does with what happens to him.

- Aldous Leonard Huxley

Change Your Thinking and You Change just about Everything

Dwelling on our failures and faults is like drinking something toxic. It eats you up on the inside and affects everything in your life on the outside. There is no purpose or benefit in exerting any of your valuable time dwelling on such thoughts, unless you are using them as stepping stones to move forward. If you can learn the lesson from your setbacks and use it in a way that motivates you to do better, then you are on the right track. Dwelling on the wrong things robs us of our vision, passion and imagination to dream again. It actually drains us of precious physical and mental energy thus making it very difficult to take action and try again. If you dwell long enough on your shortcomings and failures, they can grow into an ugly mental beast. You don't want an ugly beast running around loose in your mind. Identify the problem while it's small and get it out of your system and fast. If that beast dines on negative thinking, it's going to want to be fed every day. It craves negative thinking and the bigger it gets, the more you begin to lose emotional management. It's like having a bad renter (but in your mind). Once there, it is a struggle to have it removed.

The key for you and me is working to change our perspective on the situation. We don't have to deny the reality of it. Yet, in moving forward, we have to have a mind that is working for us. I heard a story about two guys from Montana that fell upon hard times. They decided to go hunting for wolves as the pelts of fur could be sold to pay bills and put food on the table. The first night out they had no luck in catching or coming across any wolves. So, they made camp in the wilderness, got into their tent and went to sleep. It was no more than an hour later after they had settled down for the night when they heard noises outside the tent. One of the guys unzipped the tent door, leaned out and saw close to 50 wolves surrounding them and growling. He looked at the other guy in a state of fear and said, *"We are going to die tonight."*

The other guy took a quick look outside the tent, but he did not share the same reaction as his campmate. He smiled and was filled with a positive enthusiasm. He said, *"We are not going to die tonight, we are going to be RICH!!!"*

The two hunters had different attitudes and outlooks on the situation. One found the silver lining in what could potentially be viewed as a negative situation. You have to train your mind not to ignore the negative but seek out that silver lining of positivity. It is there and it will serve you in making a way for yourself and your dreams. If you are someone who is hung up on past mistakes and failures, you have got to change your thinking and realize you can no longer control the past nor change it. It is done. It is time to use the past as a stepping stone instead of as heavy rocks in your pockets weighing you down. It is time for you to focus on the things you have influence over – your future. I like this quote: *"Do something now that your future self will be thankful for."*

"Don't wish it were easier.
Wish you were better."

- Jim Rohn

My Thinking was in the Way

I had never experienced a failure of this magnitude, one that affected so many other people besides myself. That is the part that ate me up. I never wanted to hurt anyone, but it happened and the guilt and shame was haunting. I didn't exactly have the "know how" on getting out of the mental rut I had dug for myself. I let my thinking become the enemy. The days I would try and get over it, I would get tripped up with guilt and shame. I was dwelling on every failure and thing wrong in my life. My thoughts would rabbit trail to everything wrong – I would compare myself to others, why did I have to go to kindergarten twice, why did I get picked last in third grade kickball, why did I bomb my ACT tests in high school ….and the list would go on and on. I didn't know how to shut it down. It was like Tarzan swinging from one vine to another. It would be the middle of the day and I would be emotionally and physically exhausted just because my thinking was wearing me down.

The greatest abuse I have ever known is not what anyone has done to me but what I have done to myself. I thought, *"Why try again? I am just going to fail."* Some days, all I did was sleep, eat and watch TV. I was getting lazy, overweight and disgusting. I just didn't care anymore. Someone tried to cheer me up by saying, *"Sam, keep your head up; there is light at the end of this tunnel."* I said, *"I know, it's a train coming to run me over!"* My negative thinking beast was taking over my life. I was living in a world of self-pity. I was living like a victim, turning my life into one big drama. And, it was evident to others around me. One friend in particular took some initiative and compassion to help me break the mental tread mill that I was on to help me reclaim a positive vision for my life.

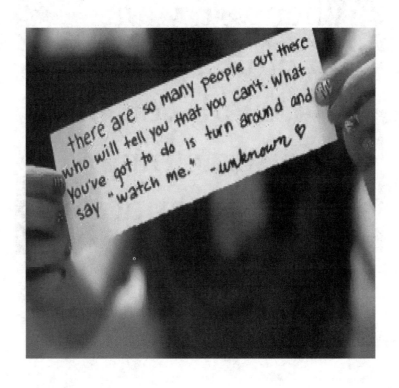

When you want something you've never had, you have to do something you've never done.

It's not your Problems that are your Problems, It's your Attitude about your Problems that is the Problem

A dear friend of many years invited me to meet up for some breakfast. I was like, *"You pay?"* He was paying and I didn't want to turn down the meal. I hung up the phone and rolled up my sleeping bag, got dressed and headed over to the restaurant. When we sat down, our conversation was mostly small talk – weather, sports, traffic and news. I felt like we just summarized the news station on Chicago AM 780. My friend took a sip of his coffee and in a different tone asked me flat out, *"How you doing for real, man?"*

I hadn't really talked to anyone about my situation or how I was feeling and thinking about myself and life. I guess my thinking led my responses to his question. Misery loves company and I was happy to share how bad my life was. I complained and vented at the rate of 100 miles per hour. I raised my voice. I took deep, loud breaths. I said that I was a victim of bad luck and bad people. It was the voice of the negative beast that that was living rent free in my mind.

I was expecting my friend to shake his head and sympathize with me a little, but he just smiled and nodded as I spoke. I started thinking, *"Why is he smiling? My life is in ruins!"*

I slowed down a little to come up for some air and my friend calmly took another sip of his coffee, looked across the table and said, *"Sam, your problems are not what the problem is. Your problem is your attitude about your problems. You just have an attitude problem."*

My first mental reaction was, *"I am going to put this guy in a head lock and dump my coffee on him! Who does he think he is telling me that I have an attitude problem?"*

He pulled out a piece of paper and a really fancy pen and said, *"Tell you what Sam. Let's make a list of everything you have to be thankful for."*

I was like *"Are you serious?"*

"Yes, I have an idea for you and think it will help you. I think if you can add up everything you have to be thankful for, you will see that your life really isn't all that bad."

I admit that I wasn't feeling particularly excited about doing this in the restaurant.

"OK Sam, what can you think of that you are thankful for?"

"Hmmmm....I don't know really."

My mind was blank and the negative thinking was trying to cut me off from thinking in any other direction. At this time in my life, I so used to playing the victim that this was a complete change of mental direction. I was so focused on all the bad that was going on with me and around me that I didn't know what to be thankful for. I just shrugged my shoulder and said, *"I really don't know. I know that sounds bad, but I don't know what to say."*

My friend continued smiling and sipping his fresh

roast coffee that seemed to be more cream than coffee, he assisted me with some suggestions. They seemed a little ridiculous at first, but once you started adding them up they made perfect sense. I needed a starting point to reboot my thinking – better thinking. If my life was going to improve, I needed to start by improving my thought patterns.

The first suggestion was *"Do you have a bed to sleep on?"*

"No, I sleep on my mom's living room floor in a sleeping bag."

"Ok, are you thankful your mom is letting you stay with her and use her floor and a sleeping bag to sleep on?"

"Yes, very much so."

"Ok…good, now write it down on the list."

The list began to grow…

Sam is thankful for:

- A place to sleep at night – mom's apartment
- A sleeping bag to sleep in
- Toothbrush
- Friends and Family who love me

- Food to eat
- A job
- Good health
- Part time transportation (we laughed at this one)
- Lived through the no brake situation
- Got to meet and get mentoring encouragement from Zig Ziglar
- Got treated to breakfast this morning
- Shoes and clothes to wear
- Peanut Butter – the smooth kind

The list grew and grew and continues to grow. I didn't just stop at what we wrote down. I gave the list a life and it continues to grow to this day.

A great life lesson: When your mind is clouded with negativity, the fastest way back into a positive perspective is to dwell on all that you have to be thankful for.

Negativity is not strong enough to hold its ground in the presence of all that is great in your life. It has to go. It has to shrink. It loses its grip and authority over your thinking. When I left the breakfast that morning, I felt like a huge weight had been lifted. I started remembering what I learned from Zig Ziglar and other great encouragers in my life. It started to flood back into my mind. Only this time, I was ready to embrace it, explore it and make it more visible in my life. We are all going to have bad days from time to time, but the bad day doesn't have to become one long drawn out permanent bad day that carries over into other days of your life. They happen and we have to deal with them and work to find a way to keep moving forward. It is just that simple: bad days happen – it's that same day whether you find yourself on the mountain top or in the valley. It is up to us to greet the day in the best possible frame of mind and of course a mouthful of peanut butter. (At the end of this book, I included a recipe for peanut butter pancakes – who can resist that? Actually, I know a person who detests peanut butter, but that is another story).

A New Kind of Famous

Gradually, the momentum of hope and purpose and positivity began to fill the cracks in my life. I could feel it. I could see it. It wasn't just a phase; it was real. Then one day, something popped into my mind after spooning up some creamy peanut butter and popping it into my mouth like a real super fan of peanut butter does. I made the BIG TIME decision to become famous. Now, I know what you might be thinking, *"Umm...that doesn't sound very humble to me Sam."*

Famous how? Like people from the movies, reality shows or sports? Nope...not even close. People are attracted to fame and the spotlight. We revel in it. But, not only did I make the choice to become famous; I also decided to redefine what fame was. I altered the definition of what famous was. Even to this day, no matter what level of success I reach (*in the eyes of others and in my own eyes*) I am always aware of where I once was and how it felt to be there. The memory of that place and who I was is permanently tattooed on my brain. It will never go away. The comments I hear over and over from fans of my work are about how I respond personally to emails with encouragement and how approachable and down to earth I am while at speaking engagements. I am not sure why people tell me this all the time, but I have never made myself out to be bigger than what I am. I have no desire to have the 15 minutes of fame that you hear about in the media all the time. That is not my kind of fame. I have finally figured it out that since the day I showed up on this planet, I have been famous every day. So are you. First and foremost, I am famous to my mom and dad. There is nobody else like me to them. I am one of a kind in this world and so that makes me pretty famous. I am an original. And, so are you.

Becoming famous for me is when I encourage someone and treat them like a rock star. You see, we can all be famous to someone every day. Being famous is how we think about ourselves and how we treat others. For example, if you do something for a customer and they love you for it, you are famous to them. You stand out. You made a positive impression that sticks with them. You have the spotlight in their minds and hearts. If you are a teacher you can be famous to a young person. If you are a manager, you can be famous to your team. If you are married, you can be famous to your spouse. This is how I define what a healthy and robust fame is. It is something we can all attain. I strive to be famous to my wife and daughter every day. I want to be someone famous to my friends and family. There are even times where we can be perceived to be famous in the eyes of someone when we do not know we are being observed by anyone. We could be the last person that individual will meet that day who can change their life for the better.

A short time ago, one of my biggest fans wrote me to sing my praises about how my books, humor and encouragement were making a difference in her life and at her workplace. Even though she was a fan, I instantly became her fan. She became famous to me because of how positive she was. She demonstrates authentic care towards people and strives every day to keep a positive workplace culture. I love that! So, one day, I decided to do something famous for her. I happened to be driving through her town from a speaking engagement and I thought I would do something famous and pay her office a surprise visit. I gave them all a copy of my latest book at the time, *The Gift of Attitude*. It was awesome! We took pictures and laughed. I shared some encouraging words and told them as I signed copies of my book, that my signature will make the book worth more when they sell it at a garage sale.

I love doing things like that to create famous experiences. It makes someone's day, puts something extra in their step and makes a positive impression that stays with them for a very long time. That super fan who I just mentioned is a really good friend now. Because she became famous to me with her encouragement and praise, I continue to strive to get better every day with my work.

A big part of being famous to me is being able to develop meaningful relationships and connections with others. When I give my speeches, you will never get the impression that I am greater or better than anyone else. I try to do for others what was done for me. Typically, when I am speaking, people feel like I am part of their family – mostly the odd ball family member. (They will think to themselves – *did he really say that??*). That is the new fame and it's something we can all achieve.

"Great minds have purposes; little minds have wishes. Little minds are subdued by misfortunes; great minds rise above them."

- Washington Irving

Sam, Would You Mind Teaching Sunday School?

A great way to redirect your thinking and shift it from negative to positive is to get involved or volunteer for a worthy cause. All the attention and focus you have on yourself shifts to helping and doing something generous for others. My brother got me involved in volunteer work with teenagers. Out of that, I was asked if I would mind teaching Sunday school a few times because the current Sunday school teacher would be away for a few weeks. I didn't mind hanging out with teenagers and encouraging them, but to actually get up in front of them and speak for an hour was a whole different ballgame. The thought of trying to hold their attention for 60 minutes made me perspire so much that I had to keep re-applying deodorant and changing my shirt. (Where's the peanut butter when you need it?) Okay, sharing that may be a little too much information, but it was for real and I was scared to say yes. I had no idea how to put a speech together. There is a statistic that says most people would prefer to die before getting up and giving a speech. I wasn't really at that point, but it was close. This was a challenge that would help me grow as a person and I wanted that for myself. The tug of war between what I wanted for myself and the fear I felt was insane. I was so nervous just thinking about it that I must have eaten a whole jar of Skippy peanut butter. I can't be sure or verify the actual information and ingredients, but I think that peanut butter must be made out of courage because I boldly took a step that I thought I would never take. I accepted the challenge. I didn't really know what to expect from this experience, but it felt good and I was excited at the prospect of defeating a lifelong lingering fear. If I flopped, I always had a little jar of Jiffy peanut butter under my bed to smooth things over.

Phone Calls and a Little Heavy Breathing

The day finally arrived for me to teach Sunday school. Surprisingly, I didn't seem to have any butterflies in my stomach. There were no butterflies in my stomach because there was no room with the all the giant size geese flying around! They ate the butterflies! I was incredibly nervous and not ready! Even though I had been working on my message for a few weeks, I still didn't feel ready, worthy or qualified to get up and speak or share a message of encouragement. My alarm sounded like a fog horn and startled me into consciousness. I sat up and began to have a panic attack. *"I can't do this! Why did I volunteer for this? I am such an idiot! I am going to call in sick."*

I plopped down in the recliner by the phone in my mom's apartment and called the church to inform them that due to some illness I would not be able to teach Sunday school. I was hoping to just leave a message so I wouldn't have to explain the illness. As luck would have it, the secretary at the church was in the office. She answered with a pleasant voice, *"Good Morning! God is Great, how can I help you this morning?"*

Now, what I am about to tell you I am not making up. I froze when she answered. I was so nervous that I was breathing rather heavily into the phone...somewhat inappropriately heavy. It didn't quite sound like a normal phone call from a normal human. I think I may have sounded like some kind of sicko weirdo! She asked very nicely, *"Excuse me. Is there something I can help you with?"*

I continued to breathe heavily into the phone and when I realized how it started sounding I hung up the phone really fast. I waited a few minutes to see if when I called back it would go to an answering machine. It didn't. I called back two more times breathing heavy and making weird sounds. I continued to give this poor secretary a reason to call the police – if she wanted.

Three times I called and I could not speak a word. I just could not talk. How weird is that? Now, I had to go teach Sunday school. When I arrived to the room where I would be conducting Sunday school, it was a full house. My first thought wasn't a good one. I thought if I started faking chest pains it might give me a reason to get out of this situation. Not my most creative idea, but I knew pulling the fire alarm might not get me much sympathy.

There must have been close to 80 teenagers who showed up for class that day. And, wouldn't you know it; they all decided to have large amounts of sugar before arriving. They were out of control. It was like mom and dad let them out of a cage back into the wild. This wasn't going to be a Bible Study as much as a safari for survival. The only adult or person in the room close to resembling an adult was me. I decided to round them all up and begin. When I opened my mouth, it sounded nothing like what I envisioned in my mind. My voice was soft, reserved and crackly, *"Hi everyone. We should probably begin. Can I have everyone come over and grab a seat?"*

Nobody was grabbing their seats or listening. So I

spoke a tad louder, *"OK, fun time is over, lets grab some wood folks!"*

Still no response. They were tossing Frisbees around like a wild day at the beach, talking, chatting, eating, and doing everything but hearing me. I was stymied. This was way worse than what I had anticipated.

I paused for a brief moment, took a giant breath of authority and found the commander and chief of my vocal box. Yelling for everyone to sit down was not something I wanted to do, so I got creative. For a split second, I squatted down like a football quarterback calling his cadence to his teammates at a tone that would break through the roar of a stadium of screaming fans.

"THREE 18! THREE 18!

BLUE! BLUE! WATCH NUMBER 58! 58!

THREE 18….SETTTTTTTTTT – HUT! HUT! GO!"

When I finished the cadence, it was silent. Everyone was silent and looking at me.

"WELCOME, NOW GRAB A SEAT AND LET'S LEARN ABOUT THE LOVE OF GOD!"

They all scrambled to grab their seats and off to the races we began. I have no clue what I talked about that day or if anything I said made any sense whatsoever.

Even when I was done, I said to myself, *"I have no clue what I just talked about."* Just as a little doubt was trying to find its way in, a few of the students came up and said, *"Mr. Glenn that was awesome! I really got something out of your lesson today. Will you be teaching again next week? Can I bring some of my friends from school? My parents forced me to come today and I am so glad they did. Mr. Glenn, why do you smell like peanut butter?"*

And, friends, that is how it all really began for me as a professional speaker. Every Sunday school after that, I opened and got everyone's attention to the football cadence. They loved it and knew that when I did it, it was time to start. The fear of public speaking was with me for a long time still, but soon it evolved into excitement. Just recently before I was introduced to speak at a banquet fundraiser, the woman sitting next to me said, *"I am so nervous for you. How can you do this? Do you ever get nervous before you speak?"*

I just laughed and said, *"You have no idea, but now it's pure excitement. I am so excited to be able to share my gifts with you."*

She smiled and said, *"That is fantastic. I think if I had to do what you do, I might pee my pants."*

I laughed, *"I think there might have been one or two times in the past few years when that may have happened to me."*

I didn't fall in love with public speaking at first. What I connected to was encouraging people who faced similar challenges as I had. I wanted to be a light to them in their darkness and get them to see that life's setbacks are really just stepping stones.

One mistake will never kill you. The same mistake over and over will.

Most of the problems in life are because of two reasons, we act without thinking or we keep thinking without acting.

Rebuilding Brick by Brick

Sometimes, the best and only option is to start over and rebuild brick by brick. When my brothers and I were growing up, we were LEGO fanatics. We would spend hours building whatever our imagination could come up with. And, as brothers and siblings like to do sometimes, we would do what I call GODZILLA the other brother's creation. We would just smash it to bits. We would work on a LEGO masterpiece for hours and hours only to have the other brother, out of anger because we would not give him the LEGO piece he needed for his creation, smash it to bits!

"MOM!!!"

"MOOOOM!!! I am telling! You jerk! You ruined my LEGO fortress and now you will pay the price!"

And after the drama simmered for a bit, we would just start over and build again brick by brick. I think it is fair to say that is how life is. Maybe you were let go from a job that you held for years and gave everything you had to. Or, like one woman I know worked several jobs to pay for her husband to go through medical school only to have him cheat on her and leave her. These are the moments we look at our life in bits and pieces and wonder how we will move forward. We have to rebuild brick by brick. I slowly began rebuilding something better for myself on the stepping stones of my past mistakes and failures. In doing that there is no guarantee that I won't battle the things I have known so well. The difference is I have more resilience and tools to win the battles faster.

Every now and then I could feel myself getting angry thinking about the people that were dishonest and who had burned me in some way. I wanted to find these people and pull their underwear over their heads. I think that's called an over-the-head wedgie. I used to practice on my brothers all the time. I thought about it but never did it. Thinking about such things was a waste of time— a trap. I needed to be free of that kind of thinking. But, I still think it would be a good life rule that when someone is rude and dishonest, we should be able to give them an over-the-head wedgie. It's fun to imagine.

Rebuilding brick by brick, I started to put a greater emphasis on making healthy and empowering choices. I was more aware of the decisions I was making. I tried to go for walks to relieve stress. I didn't watch as much TV. I ate less donuts and junk food, and I started eating better foods for energy. And, despite what your thoughts are on peanut butter, it is still with me but in moderation. (Are you waiting for the peanut butter pancake recipe?) I began to read and listen to any book on audio that I could afford. I didn't go to the library to get books, because I wanted to read them over and over and take notes and mark them up with highlights. So, I tried to keep my eyes open for good books at good discounts. I didn't have a bank roll flowing in, so I needed to be on the lookout for good deals. I also wrote in a journal so I could track my progress. As I did these things, I could feel the courage growing inside me to venture out and act on my gifts and talents. They were no good sitting around, so I was about to give them some life.

YOUR LIFE WILL FOLLOW THE DIRECTION OF YOUR
MOST DOMINANT THOUGHTS, SO CHOOSE THE KIND OF
THINKING THAT WILL BE POSITIVE FOR YOUR LIFE.

Not Everyone will Buy into your Dreams and Ideas....AT FIRST!

The vision I had for myself moving forward was to explore the world of professional speaking. Nobody knew who I was and so I had no credibility to open doors. Even today, there are a lot of people who have no idea who I am, but word of mouth is substantial. It is the reason we continue to grow and thrive. The best marketing is an excellent job.

I had no prospects or marketing budget. And, since I was still sleeping on my mom's living room floor, it was hard for some to buy into the idea of me becoming a motivational speaker. I wasn't exactly like Chris Farley's character on SNL - Matt Foley – a motivational speaker who lives in a van down by the river. I lived in a sleeping bag on the floor of my mom's apartment. I guess it had some similarities, but I recall one person saying to me, *"What are you going to motivate people to do –stop sleeping on the floor?"*

I wasn't negative or reactive to their inquiry, I simply said, *"Yes, because I will be speaking from experience. There are a lot of people who have experienced hardships like me and they can relate to me and me to them. My goal is to help people see how relevant their attitude is in perseverance and resilience when life lays you out flat. A lot of people are lying on the ground mentally and want to give up. I want to encourage them, like the people who have encouraged me, to rise again and live the life they were meant to live."*

My topic of choice was ATTITUDE. It is a broad topic and just about everyone under the sun talks about attitude in some way, shape or form. However, I chose the topic of attitude specifically because it was and has always been my biggest struggle. I happen to believe the topic of attitude picked me to be a messenger. I really do. One aspect I love about this topic is its relevance. I have taken the concept of attitude and given it a fresh perspective. People connect with the message and want to hear more. I didn't just randomly pick the topic of attitude out of a hat. I found my purpose in it. I knew I would not be speaking from a theoretical standpoint but from a reality standpoint. My attitude was and is a constant challenge that requires daily maintenance. I might even say that my attitude is high maintenance. I have to work on it daily, and if I don't, negativity will seep in and complicate my life.

I was already a world class renowned expert on being negative, so I had that side of the coin covered. I knew first hand that companies don't like to hire people with negative attitudes. It is hard to get promoted and move up in an organization with a negative attitude. It's hard to make sales when you are negative. It's hard to have loyal customers when you treat others with a negative attitude. A negative attitude doesn't put money in your bank account. A negative attitude doesn't attract the right person or relationships into your life. A negative attitude doesn't fuel dreams to become a reality. I was already an expert on this side of the attitude coin. In my journey to overcome the stranglehold of negative thinking, I began to research and learn how to use my attitude towards a different purpose. It is a never ending classroom that is never routine or boring. I might say it's rather adventurous.

Input creates output. If you don't like the output in your life – meaning your attitude and actions, then you need to change your input – what you read, who you spend time with and those things you permit to influence your life.

DON'T BE AFRAID TO SIT IN THE FRONT ROW AT YOUR LIFE.

Lottery Tickets Don't Pay the Bills! Ya Gotta Do The Work!

It was a new day and a fresh start. I used to run across the street from my mom's apartment complex to a 7-11 where I would buy scratch off lottery tickets in hopes of changing my situation if I won. It never happened Now, I was buying newspapers to find a job so I could start paying back some of the money I owed people and to help my mom with some of her living expenses. I grabbed a paper and some Peter Pan peanut butter (you see, I like all brands) and set off to browse the classified listings.

One job listing for a nighttime janitor caught my eye. It required all sorts of janitorial services for office buildings around the Chicago metro area. It was also the graveyard shift. It would work perfectly because I could work nights for them and then work on my dream of being a national speaker by day. I quickly called the company, Skyline Janitorial Services, and after a brief conversation they asked if I would be willing to come in that day to interview. I put on a nice shirt, my best slacks and made my way to their offices. When the interview started, I felt it fair to be up front with the person doing the hiring about my vision of becoming a motivational speaker. I explained that I would like the job because during the days I would be working on my new business. Surprisingly, he was very supportive that I had such a goal. He even said that if there was anything he could do to encourage me in the pursuit of my goals to let him know. I was hired on the spot. The owner of the company handed me two double extra-large Skyline T-shirts to wear on the job and a schedule of when to show up to begin training. I felt good about this step in my rebuilding plan. It was a start. It was a humbling start, but it was a start. It's like this: *"You don't have to be great to start, but if you want to become great you need to start."*

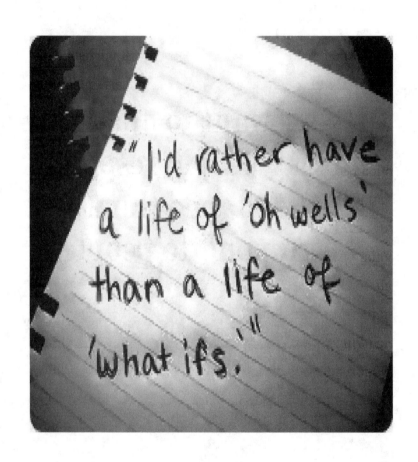

If you want to change the way people respond to you, change the way you respond to people.

Dunkin Donuts Coffee Shop Saves The Day

Nobody said the graveyard shift would be easy. It took me a while to get acclimated to the time change and sleep deprivation. I would show up for work about 7 P.M. and by midnight I was ready to find a spot anywhere to lie down and sleep. I must have drunk two large cups of Dunkin Donuts coffee every night to keep going.

My routine was set. I would work 9 to 13 hours a night, go back to my mom's apartment, crawl into my sleeping bag and sleep a few hours. I would get up and prepare to call potential clients letting them know who I was and what I do.

"Hello?"

"Hi, my name is Sam Glenn and I was wondering if

you guys ever do events and have motivational speakers?"

"Ummm yes. Why?"

"Well, I am an inspirational speaker who ignites people with passion to persevere and use their attitude to make a way when there seems like there is no way. I was wondering if you would be interested in getting some information? Ummm...are you still there? Hello? Hello? Hmm....we must have got disconnected."

I didn't quite have a solid sales pitch that peaked people's interests. It was apparent that most of my calls were an interruption to most people's day. But, the only way I could get hired was if people knew that I was available to be hired, and I knew they would love my presentations. I endured some rejection, got disconnected, hung up on, screamed at and encouraged to jump off a bridge. I thought it was kind of odd that the pastor of my church would tell me to jump off a bridge. But, hey! I am kidding; he didn't really tell me that. One lady, however, did say, *"Sir, stop calling and while you are at it maybe you could jump off a bridge!!!"* That inspired me more because I thought, *"WOW, with an attitude like that, they really need a speaker on attitude!"*

I even enlisted the help of my 80-something-year-old grandma. She would label up postcards and mail them out to organizations to book me to speak. It's kind of funny, but in my grandma's retirement community they have happy hour around 4 P.M. – just about every day. It's a time to be social and put a few martinis back. Grandma loved happy hour and I think after one (very happy) happy hour, she decided to work on my postcards. She labeled up 500 of them and dropped them in the mail. She called and told me she got 500 out in the mail and to let her know if anyone calls to hire me to speak. Grandma was a hard worker and wanted to see me be successful. This particular time, however, she labeled up 500 postcards and mailed them all to me. She mixed up the labels. For a week, I got 500 postcards encouraging me to hire me. I didn't get mad, but rather I had a good laugh and thought, *"I would hire me! (Lord, where is the peanut butter when you need it)."*

My mother said to me, "if you become a solider, you'll be a general; if you become a monk, you'll end up as the Pope.' So, I became a painter and wound up as Picasso."

– Pablo Picasso

Time is Flying By and Still Nothing is Happening

For the better part of a year, the only results I got from my marketing efforts were high phone bills. That was my biggest expense. Mom was kind enough to let me stay with her for nearly three years. Those three years my mom and I developed a special relationship. Even though she was unsure of things in the beginning, she eventually became my biggest all-star fan.

When nobody would call me back, I didn't know what to do. I got desperate one day and started leaving messages for people, *"A biker, a priest and a rabbi walk into a bar. If you want to hear the rest of the joke, call me back at #######"*

Yeah, that didn't work either. Nobody was calling me back to have me speak to their organization. This didn't look promising, but I stayed the course. I continued working nights as a janitor, and by day, I worked on the dream and not making weird phone calls to people.

On the Clock...

The pressure started growing around me to put my dream of being a professional speaker on hold for a little while and get a 9 to 5 job. It was a mental war. Working nights as a janitor provided some income but not enough to live on. I didn't listen to good wisdom when I was running my Grandpa's business. In recalling that, I felt that maybe I should take the advice of others this time. I didn't want to let anyone else down or be blinded by my ambitions again. So after about a year of doing everything I could to get my speaking career off the ground, I succumbed to the pressure and reluctantly dusted off my resume and submitted it to as many companies I could.

My cover letter was **10 Reasons You Should Hire Sam Glenn**. I got immediate call backs from some great organizations. One happened to be a mortgage company based in downtown Chicago. I went in for the interview and they loved me. They loved my attitude, my energy and my passion for success. Only this time I didn't share my vision and dream of wanting to be a motivational speaker. Oddly enough, the guy who interviewed me said, *"Wow, I like your attitude Sam. You are positive, energetic and got what we are looking for."*

Jokingly he added, *"If anything, you can motivate the rest of the staff here. You could make a great motivational speaker if this doesn't work out."*

When he said that I could feel my heart beat really hard.

The next day, they called to offer me a job. I put in my notice at the janitorial company and accepted the new position at this mortgage company. Everyone who encouraged me to go this route with my life was happy for me, *"Sam, this is the right thing to do. Work on getting some stability and when the time is right in 5 or 10 years, you can take up professional speaking again."*

Since I lived in Naperville, I was about to learn and develop a whole new appreciation for people who commute to work. In fact, that may be the toughest part of their job – the commute. Either way, I tip my hat to you. I had to catch a crowded bus to the crowded train station. It took me about a good hour and some to get down to the city. I remember thinking, *"How do people do this every day?"* It was crowded everywhere you went and everyone was in a rush. I just wasn't acclimated to this kind of process, so it all was a whirlwind of craziness for me. I didn't see one happy face, including mine. Correction, I did see one happy face. It was some guy who was talking to himself and he seemed like it was the best conversation of his life. For a moment, I was wondering if we were related.

I had a stomachache because I felt like I had given up on my dream. It felt like when my brothers would knock over my LEGO creations. I was back to the starting point again. Or, so it felt.

what
comes
easy,
won't last,
what
lasts,
won't
come easy.

I Got the Burger King Blues

My first day on the job was all training. The attitude I had shown up with at the interview wasn't the same that day. A few people asked me if I was sick or not feeling well. I didn't' feel well about this choice. It was prodding me with a sense of regret. I could hardly focus on the training because my mind was still working hard on the dream. It was conditioned to work on my dream everyday with no excuses, so my mind was still working on the job that I had just left.

For lunch, I walked like a zombie three blocks to a crowded Burger King. It was the only thing I could afford, so it worked. I ordered a cheeseburger, fries and water. I sat down on a seat that just opened up and still had crumbs lingering on the table. I set my tray of food down and just starred at it. I just slumped over in my seat trying as hard as I could not to cry or tear up. I wanted this dream so bad and I had turned my life around and recovered from failure, adversity and fears. I had come so far and yet at that moment, fighting back the tears, all I could feel was that familiar feeling of being a failure again.

Hypnotized by Blah, Blah, Blah

I was in what I call a blah mood the rest of the day. Blah is a feeling of being out of it, blue, or just dazed. I was hypnotized by blah. I don't remember the train and bus ride home other than that it was crowded and everyone looked like zombies. My mom asked me with a sense of enthusiasm how my first day was on the new job. She was happy for me because getting that job would lead to some stability for me. I didn't want to lead her on about my feelings, so I acted really tired and let her know it was all good.

When Mom went to bed that night, I stayed up, sat on the floor and rested my back up against the couch and my mind began to have a wrestling match – *what do I do?* It also seemed weird not to be getting ready to go do janitorial work. I was happy that I didn't have to but it was a new feeling because usually it was about that time when I was getting ready to head in for a full night of work.

I could not sleep. I would turn on the TV for a bit and then would turn it off. I did this a few times. There was a wrestling match going on in my mind and I couldn't find any rest.

I lifted myself a little off the ground to look over the couch to see what time it was on the microwave clock. Ugh -it was a little after 2 A.M.. I had to be up in three hours to get ready for work. I didn't want to go. I knew in my heart that if I went to work the next day I would get up and be going to that job for a very long time as my dream was shrinking. I had listened to everyone's advice and opinions about getting this job, but it didn't seem right. I wasn't blinded by my ambitions like I was with my grandpa's business, but rather I had some wisdom and a real vision of where I wanted to go. I wasn't sure exactly how to get there, but I knew without a doubt that I was going there.

The other issue was if I got up and went to that job my heart would not be in it. That would not be right and it would be unfair to the organization. The scariest person in my opinion is the person who doesn't care and shows up to work anyway. I didn't want that to be me. I knew they would not get my best.

The other factor was that there was no guarantee when something might happen if I stayed the course of my dreams. It could be days, weeks or years and that could be difficult to explain to those who love me and have my best interest at hand. I had worked for almost a year on my dream and did the right things, made the right choices, and still nobody had called me to come speak to their group yet. However, I knew in my gut that if I continued with this new job, I would end up killing all the momentum I had built up for my dream.

BEING POSITIVE IN A NEGATIVE SITUATION IS NOT NAIVE. IT'S LEADERSHIP.

Time to Eat Some
Faith and Courage Stew

PHILIPPIANS 4

⁴ Always be full of joy in the Lord; I say it again, rejoice! ⁵ Let everyone see that you are unselfish and considerate in all you do. Remember that the Lord is coming soon. ⁶ Don't worry about anything; instead, pray about everything; tell God your needs and don't forget to thank him for his answers. ⁷ If you do this you will experience God's peace, which is far more wonderful than the human mind can understand. His peace

I made my decision. It didn't come easy, but I knew what I had to do. I was about to do something that would feed my faith in achieving my dream and my courage to keep moving forward. Quietly, I extended my arm to pick up the phone. Every number I pressed I could feel my heart beating rapidly and my breathing picking up as well too. The phone started ringing and I was able to get my boss's voice mail. *Please leave a message at the sound of the tone.*

"Hi, this is Sam Glenn. I want to thank you for the opportunity you gave me in hiring me to work for your company. But, I can't work for you at this time. It's difficult to explain. I am deeply sorry for any inconvenience. I hope you understand."

Click.

I sat back down on the floor, stared off into the darkness in the room and it began to sink in: I was all in. This was the real deal. I had to prove to my family that I hadn't lost my mind by making this choice. I believed it was the best choice for me, but I did feel a little scared that I was now walking on pure faith. Faith is having hope everything will work out for the best despite everything being a mystery.

The Longest Two Weeks Ever

Two weeks passed from when I made that late night call to tell my boss that I would not be returning to work. Those were two very scary weeks. They may have been the longest two weeks of my life. I was trying to do everything I could to make something happen. I was all in. I even started stalking the phone and answering machine hoping it would ring with anyone wanting information or to talk with me about speaking to their group. My fingers were crossed that something or anything would happen. It had to, and so on. I was down to my last few dollars and it wasn't looking too promising. I worked on myself, my message and letting people know who I was and what I did. I got hung up on, yelled at, asked not to call again and lots of voicemails.

Despite all that rubbish that would justify doubt, my dream was stronger and kept pulling me forward.

It was approximately 12:48 in the afternoon. I had just made a cup of coffee and listening to the brew of the coffee machine. I glanced outside and it was a beautiful day. The skies were blue with just a few clouds that looked like giant out-of-shape cotton balls. I could hear the local birds chirping as they played. I was running through my checklist of things I needed to get done that day. I was thinking that before I went out I needed to take a quick shower. I poured my coffee, added some cream and took it with me into the bathroom. *Time to get ready to go out and make some contacts.*

I started the shower. While it was warming up, I picked up a book that I had left in there and read a positive quote. I smiled and shook my head up-and-down in a positive agreement, *"I like that one! That is a good quote."*

I love positive quotes and read them all the time. The shower was ready and as I was putting my first foot in over the tub it happened. I turned my head to be sure I was hearing what I was hearing right. It was the phone! It was ringing. I was trying to put some clothes on as fast as I could to run out and answer it, but I wasn't fast enough. I reached out for the phone and may have even said really loud, *"Wait!!!!"*

I missed the call, but the answering machine picked up. I didn't know if it would be for my mom, my brother, a bill collector, telemarketer or someone who wanted me to speak to their group. I calmly got to the phone and listened as whoever was calling started to leave a message.

"Hi, I was calling for Sam Glenn. Sam, this is -------, we got your materials a while back and were wondering if you would like to come speak to about 50 or so teachers. If they like you, they may invite you to their schools to speak. We don't have a budget to pay you, but we want to spice up our meeting with something different and you seem to fit the bill. Let us know if you can do it. Please call us back when you can."

My eyes got gigantic as I listened to the message. I played it over and over and howled with excitement, *"YES!!!!!!!! Yes! Yes! Yes!"*

It felt comforting and exciting that something that I wanted was happening. I was so excited and called them back. Ten minutes later, I had my first, official speaking engagement. I didn't even care that they weren't paying me. It was something to build on.

Great things never came from comfort zones.

If It Can Go Wrong, It Will Go Wrong So What Do You Do?

The day of the event had come. It was my first real speaking engagement. A year had gone by and was filled with rejection and criticism, but this is what living your dream is all about. Who cares that I slept on my mom's floor? Who cares that I was down to my last few dollars? Who cares what negative people think? I was doing it! I had a hope, meaning and purpose. Nothing could mess up this day!

The event was two hours from where I lived. I loaded up my '82 Buick Regal and set out on my way. I wasn't exactly sure if my car would make it to the event. I tried not to think about it. Betty, that's what I called my car, was older and she had just started leaking oil.

Sometimes it took a little time to get her started and she would make some smells that didn't seem healthy for a reliable car. And if you got her up to 60 miles per hour, she would start to shake and vibrate so much that it felt like you were reentering the earth's atmosphere from space. Despite my concerns, I kept a positive attitude that everything would work out and all would be okay.

As I got closer to the event location, Starved Rock Lodge located in Starved Rock, Illinois, everything seemed to be going smoothly. Betty wasn't shaking too badly and I was making good time. Actually, I was making really good time. By my estimate, I would be there almost five hours early. I wanted to have some extra time to go over my notes for my speech and calm my nerves a bit. I wanted to make a good impression so they would invite me to speak to their schools and tell others about me.

I saw my exit off Interstate 80 and as I hit the turn signal to exit, I noticed the gas light pop on. I was almost out of gas. That wasn't the bad part. The bad part was when I pulled into the gas station to get gas, I couldn't find my wallet. Have you ever left the house on a trip or for the day and have that feeling you forgot something? I had that feeling, but I seemed to have what I needed. That is, everything but my wallet. My wallet wasn't bursting with cash and credit, but there was enough to get the gas I needed for the day. My good friend who sat down with me over a cup of coffee to create a grateful list had given me a few dollars to help keep me going. When I told him I wasn't getting paid for the event, but that my dream was coming true, he was generous enough to support me by giving me a few dollars. In fact, he gave me a book, "Tough Times Don't Last, But Tough People Do". He gave it to me to fuel my momentum to keep going. I had turned everything around and he was excited and could visually see it compared to that day at the coffee shop.

I was so glad I cracked that book open and started reading it. He placed a gift of $300 cash inside the pages. That is what I earned in two weeks of work as a janitor, and for someone to give that to me with no expectation other than me making something good happen in my life was awesome. But, I had forgotten my wallet that had the money to help pay for gas. A lesson to note is that if it can go wrong, it will go wrong. The question is how will you respond to what goes wrong? How you respond is the most important thing. I shook my head and began to panic. I scrambled to find $1.56 in my car on the floor, under the seats and a penny on the ground outside my door. I lifted the nozzle and carefully put in $1.56 worth of gas into Betty. When I went to pay, the cashier asked me, *"Did you have trouble getting gas out? Is that why you only put in $1.56?"*

"No, I only had $1.56."

She nodded like she understood. I had enough gas to make it the rest of the way but not nearly enough to get home. I wasn't sure what I would do, but I needed to get to the event location and get ready.

The Worst Speech Ever Became Someone's Best Speech Ever

I pulled up to the Starved Rock Lodge, parked and quickly turned off Betty. For some reason I kept looking at the gas gauge, hoping that I was reading it wrong and it really wasn't empty. Betty was down to just a few more sips of gas and then we would be empty. I didn't want any distractions today, but the thought of how I was going to get home kept lingering in my mind. It kept interrupting my focus. It was frustrating.

The time came to speak. I didn't tell anyone about my gas problem and tried to act like nothing was wrong. I needed to do a good job so people would hire me to speak. I was standing off to the side. Since I didn't have a lot of credentials, my introduction was maybe about three sentences long.

"...Let's give Sam Glenn an enthusiastic welcome!"

I walked up to the microphone and the first few words out of my mouth sounded jumbled like a bad sneeze. My mouth was so dry that it looked like I was chewing on cotton balls during my speech. (No, I did not have a mouthful of peanut butter. It was embarrassing. I was nervous and had put so much pressure on myself to do a good job that everything was a distraction. My words and sentences at times didn't really make sense. I tried to recover a few times, but as I looked at everyone watching me, I saw a familiar look on everyone's face. In high school, I had to take a speech class. Because I got so nervous, I didn't make much sense during my speeches. The class would have this look on their face, *"This poor guy is sinking, making no sense. He looks scared and doesn't know what he is talking about."*

My speech wasn't going well. If there was an award for the worst speech ever, I was about to achieve it. I would start telling a story and then get to a place and forget what to say next. My recovery was mumbled as I tried to sound somewhat coherent. Then I heard a voice in my head,

"Sam you are stinking! They hate you! Look at their faces. Everyone is yawning. People are looking out the window. Your speech made them want to jump out the window. "

It was literally the worst speech ever! When I was done, the audience clapped with more sympathy than excitement. You could read it on their expressions that it wasn't a good segment for them. There was a short break for the group after my speech and everyone got up and left the room. Nobody said thanks or shook my hand. Nobody looked at the business cards that I had laid out on the back table. It hit me fast. It hit me hard. I thought I was going to be sick. I started to feel doubt working its way into my thinking. It wasn't a good sign.

Focus on your goal.

Don't look in any direction but ahead.

It Wasn't a Failure,
It was a Stepping Stone

I finished the speech, gathered my notes and quickly walked down the hallway past people who had just heard my speech. I made a quick stop in the restroom and hid out in the big stall for a little bit. I didn't want anyone to see me. It was a quick escape. I could hear two guys engaging in a conversation at the counter as they washed their hands, *"What did you think of that session?"*

"I felt bad for the guy. Why was he eating cotton balls during his speech?"

I stayed in the big stall in the bathroom until it was time for them to go back to their meeting room and nobody could see me. I didn't want anyone to find me or know I was there. With the sounds of toilets flushing every few minutes, I could hear my dream flushing as I began to beat myself up mentally. *"Sam, you should just quit. You worked an entire year on this dream and this is what you do - fail! You are going to live with your mom forever, sleeping on her floor. You are the worst speaker ever. You are a failure."*

As I was walking briskly to my car, Betty, I heard someone call out to me, *"Excuse me, Sam! Can I talk with you?"*

I wasn't sure what he wanted and actually thought he was going to criticize my speech or put me down in some way. I mean, I did give him a reason too. My speech was a train wreck.

"Sam, hey, I was looking for you and wanted to thank you for your presentation today. Sam, I need to let you know. I didn't want to come to this event today. I laid in bed for an hour staring at the walls trying to find a reason to get up. I have been pretty depressed as of late. I recently got a divorce and never get to see my kids. It's been tough. But, today, I got something powerful from your message and I want to thank you for that. You gave me some much needed hope. I am so glad that I came now. I would only leave you with this, don't stop doing what you are doing; you are going to touch

the lives of a lot of people with the gift of who you are."

I was in shock. I thought I had failed and it made my day when he told me that. It cleared the debris of negative thinking. It wasn't a failure. It was the sign of my harvest. It was a dream coming to my life.

The guy walked away with tears in his eyes. It was obvious that if I had given up, I would not be at that point and time to help encourage someone under the weight of their adversity. He was the reason I wanted to pursue and do what I was doing. It made a difference for one person. That has to count for something; doesn't it? It wasn't the greatest batting average, but it had to count for something. So, the speech didn't go well; is that enough reason to give up? Should it be enough? No way. I could learn from this... grow from this... become more from this. Failure is my stepping stone.

"Start by doing what is necessary, then do what is possible, and suddenly you are doing the impossible."

- St. Francis of Assisi

My $100 Miracle!!!

That was a powerful moment for me and my dream. It continues to be a moment that I love sharing with audiences. But, the fact still remained; I didn't have enough gas to get home from the event. I unlocked the door, sat down in the driver's seat and began to think of what I could do. It was warm out, so I left the car door wide open and let my left leg dangle out the side. I reached my hand down between the seats to see if I might find some loose change by chance. I looked outside on the ground - nothing. I needed a miracle. As I was letting out a heavy breath, I heard someone shout my name, *"Sam! Wait! Hold on! Don't go yet!"*

Little did they know, I wasn't going anywhere. It was the guy who I just had a conversation with about how my speech gave him some hope. He was walking towards me really fast and when he got within arm's length reached down and put something in my pocket.

"Sam, here is a little something. It's not much, but a small gift that I want you to have. Keep up the good work. You are going to touch a lot of lives. You have safe travels home. I have to get back into the session, so God Bless."

He walked away and his words of encouragement simmered in my mind. By the time he reached the door of the Lodge, I was reaching down and looking down to see what he had put in my pocket. I pulled out a $10 bill! That was more than enough to gas up my car and get me home! Since I had done something for him, I think he wanted to give me a gift. That was nice and a small miracle.

I drove to the gas station, put $10 of gas into Betty and walked in to pay for the gas. As I walked to the door, I reached into my pocket to get the $10 bill and when I pulled it out there was more currency with it. The guy didn't just put $10 in my pocket. That was all I had pulled out. Coupled with the $10 bill in my hand was a brand new $100 bill. My eyes just about popped out as I stared at it to make sure I was seeing it right. He gave me a gift of $110. I felt a rush of excitement in my chest and had a smile so big that I had to treat myself to a coke and peanut butter cookies.

From that moment, I have never looked back. I have been speaking full time for a long time now. Has it been an easy journey? No way. But, the power of perseverance and the power of encouragement have made the difference. You have what it takes to do great things with your life. You may fail big along the way and that is okay. Failure can propel us to places we never could have even imagined.

On the other side of that territory is the land of dreams coming true. So, the next time you get rejected, criticized, challenged and collide with failure

– GET EXCITED! You know that you are on your way! It's a sign. You've entered the land that lies just at the borders of your dream! Ask yourself, *"Is your dream worth continuing on for?"*

My hope is your answer is a big, *"YES!"*

Well
DONE
IS BETTER THAN
WELL SAID

BENJAMIN FRANKLIN

Valuable Lessons I Learned
that Have
Become My Stepping Stones

•Find people who you trust and believe in you. Surround yourself with their encouragement. Dismiss those who bring you down. People will either bring out your best or your worst. You choose who you surround yourself with. Stick with the winners.

•Look for the best in every adverse situation. Try to find the lesson learned. That lesson learned will become your stepping stone.

•Find others who can help you get through whatever adversity you are facing. They may give you the ideas and suggestions that will provide you with the solutions you need.

•Talk to yourself in a positive way. When we walk through adversity, rejection, failure and criticism, we tend to beat up ourselves. Take time to do an inventory of all your victories – even the smallest of them. Remind yourself of why your dream is valuable to you. Encourage yourself, because at times you just might be the only one around to do so. Don't feed your insecurities and fears with toxic words or excuses. Use words that have life and energy: *"I can do this. This too shall pass. I am valuable and make a difference."* Find the right words that work best for you. Check out my Facebook page to support you. Write them down and carry them on a note card in your pocket or purse because in the midst of adversity, it's easy to forget the words that inspire perseverance.

•Keep a journal. You will want to remember good times and tough moments. Record what you learn. Record your thoughts, fears, ideas, goals, solutions, and whatever you want. I have found it is so encouraging to look back and see where I was and how far I have come. Chart the course of where you want to go, who you want to become, and what you want to have.

•Get involved in a worthy cause that takes the focus off you and puts it on helping others. This is one of the most empowering ways to feel good about yourself and your contributions.

•Educate yourself with the skills your desired craft requires. Keep improving and bettering yourself. Invest in your future. You are worth it! Education is the most dynamic way to build confidence and greater self-esteem. Read. Listen. Ask. Seek. Find. Discover. Invest. Do whatever it takes to grow and keep learning. Life is an awesome classroom.

•Lose the excuses. *"If only this, if only that, that person did this, the economy this, my spouse that, yada, yada, yada"* …All excuses are from the defeated mentality library. If something is bothering you, change what you can, and let go of the rest.

•Stop the pity parties. Stop dwelling on your defeats and celebrate each new positive step forward in your life – even the small ones.

•It's not what happens to us that matters but how we deal with what happens to us. You might have to rebuild, start over, forgive, and find new reasons to get up in the morning. The key is to do just that. Start! Start to rebuild, forgive, and find reasons to keep going. I love the line from Tom Hanks in the movie Castaway, *"I am going to get up one day at a time and just breathe."* He had to start his life over again and, simply put, decided to start by breathing first. That is a good place to start, because the storms often knock the wind out of us.

•Look for the humor in your situations. Despite the setbacks and twists in the road, I was able to laugh and the laughter helped me keep a positive perspective and eliminate unnecessary stress.

Complete LIFE's LITTLE Instruction B...

Never give up on anybody. Miracles happen every day.

GRATITUDE
TURNS
WHAT
WE
HAVE
INTO
ENOUGH

A Positive Note on Which to End

I will wrap this book up with a good story. I told you this story ends in a very positive way. My story is not as bad as some that have been shared with me over the years. It's more of a story of personal discovery and education. There have been some hard times along the way and moments when I felt the life got knocked out of me. But, I found a way to keep going. I am not sure what will happen tomorrow, but I know one thing, for sure, I will find a way to keep going. I just read an article about the victims of the Boston Marathon bombing that happened a few years ago. Despite what happened, the article was all about each of them and how they are finding a way to use the experience as a positive stepping stone. They didn't ask for what happened to happen; it just occurred without any warning or notice. That is just how most of adversity works. As I read the article and the stories of each of the victims, I was inspired to appreciate my own life and follow their example of finding the stepping stone in life's unexpected potholes.

Looking back, if my grandfather's business hadn't been lost, I would not be doing what I am doing today. Some of my closest and most encouraging friends are people I have met through my speeches and books. Had I stopped caring, I know I would still be lost. But, I was lucky to have a few good people who encouraged me with gentle love and tough love to help me make better choices for myself.

The good story on the broken road of my life is that

it led me to meet someone special, who I married and together we have been blessed with the most beautiful little girl ever. Well, my wife did most of the having part as I looked on with weird faces. But, it was something that I wasn't sure would ever happen for me. When I look at my daughter now, I can say that she makes the trip worth it. I would walk the broken road barefoot knowing she was waiting for me. She is my prize for not giving up. My wife and I plan to have more kids one day, and when we do, the ending of this book will change because I want them to feel as special. I want my daughter to be inspired by my stories, because I am learning as a new dad that I can't protect my daughter from everything. She has to go out into the real world one day and grow from her own bumps and bruises. My hope is that she will learn from my story and use the lessons to make smart choices and be inspired when life throws her a curve ball to have the heart to keep moving forward and to use her setbacks as positive stepping stones. My hope is that this book will become her peanut butter. Speaking of peanut butter, I think we may be out so I need to run out and grab some.

Thank you for taking the time to read my book and

hear my story. Keep moving forward!

As promised, here is the peanut butter pancake recipe that I found on Google. Right now I am thinking about making up a batch for myself! One of these days, I hope we meet and can exchange stories. I would be truly blessed if I knew that my life experiences have helped you in any fashion. If you have the time, drop me a note or visit me at: www.SamGlenn.com .

Peanut Butter Pancakes Recipe

This recipe is from Rachael Ray, *minus the "kid" part of making the pancakes into poodles. Surprisingly, the pancakes were good – a little heavy, but that's to be expected with peanut butter. Next time, I'm adding sliced bananas.*

- **Peanut Butter Pancake Ingredients**
- 1 ¼ cups flour
- 2 tablespoons sugar
- 2 ½ teaspoons baking powder
- ½ teaspoon salt
- 1 ¼ cups milk
- 1 large egg
- ¼ cup peanut butter
- 3 tablespoons butter, melted

In a large bowl, whisk together the flour, sugar, baking powder and salt. In a small bowl, beat together the milk, egg, peanut butter and butter until smooth. Pour the wet ingredients into the dry and stir until just combined.

Heat a nonstick griddle or large nonstick skillet over medium heat. Spoon out 1/4 cup batter onto the griddle for each pancake. Cook until pancake begins to puff and the bottom is golden, about 2 minutes. Flip and cook until golden on the other side. Repeat with the remaining batter.

"Rest if you must, but don't give up on yourself or your dreams. Make something great happen for yourself and in doing so, you will make incredible things happen for others as well. Make your time count! I believe the best is yet to come for you....so be on the look out!"

— Sam Glenn, The Attitude Guy

About Sam Glenn

The Attitude Guy ©

With Sam Glenn, *"It's all about attitude!"* Sam went from working nights as a janitor – negative, depressed, uptight and sleeping on the floor – to discovering his calling. With that he has found happiness, humor and a king size Serta mattress. They say the two most memorable moments of any event are the opening and the closing. Sam Glenn is widely known as one of the most entertaining and energizing speakers to kick off conferences and wrap them up. At one time, Sam's most terrifying fear was public speaking; years later, he has won multiple awards for his speeches, having been named Speaker of the Year by several organizations and spoken to audiences as large as 75,000 people at stadium events. Today, Sam delivers close to 100 uplifting speeches a year to organizations and conference events that focus on recharging people's attitude batteries. As Sam humorously likes to share, *"I don't use PowerPoint in my presentations. I don't need it. I have ADHD, which means —I am the PowerPoint!"*

Sam and his family, originally from Stillwater, Minnesota, currently reside in Carmel, Indiana. In his free time, he likes to fish, collect funny stories and practice anger management skills on the golf course. Sam is always grateful for word of mouth endorsement, so if you enjoyed this book and know someone who might benefit from it, please spread some attitude by telling others.

More Books by Sam Glenn – *Get One!*

www.SamGlennBooks.com